With All Thy Mind

Worship That Honors the Way God Made Us

Robert P. Glick

THE
ALBAN
INSTITUTE
Herndon, Virginia
www.alban.org

The Alban Institute
2121 Cooperative Way, Suite 100
Herndon, VA 20171

Scripture quotations, unless otherwise noted, are from the Holy Bible, New International Version, copyright © 1973, 1978, 1984, International Bible Society, and are used by permission of Zondervan Publishing House.

Scripture quotations marked RSV are from the Revised Standard Version of the Bible, copyright © 1946, 1952, 1971, by the Division of Christian Education of the National Council of the Churches of Christ in the United States of America and are used by permission.

Scripture quotations marked NRSV are from the New Revised Standard Version of the Bible, copyright © 1989, Division of Christian Education of the National Council of Churches of Christ in the United States of America and are used by permission.

Scripture quotations marked ESV are from the English Standard Version of the Bible, copyright © 2001, by the Standard Bible Society. Used by permission.

Scripture quotations marked KJV are from the King James Version of the Bible and are used by permission.

Cover design by Wendy Ronga, Hampton Design Group.

Library of Congress Cataloging-in-Publication Data

Glick, Robert P.
  With all thy mind : worship that honors the way God made us / Robert P. Glick.
      p. cm. — (Vital worship, healthy congregations series)
  Includes bibliographical references.
  ISBN-13: 978-1-56699-324-1
  ISBN-10: 1-56699-324-5
  1. Public worship—Psychology. 2. Brain—Religious aspects—Christianity. I. Title. II. Series.

  BV15.G55 2006
  264.001'9—dc22
                                    2006008816

13   12   11   10   9   8   7   6   UG   1   2   3   4   5   6   7

This book is fondly dedicated
to all the hard-core right-brain and left-brain
thinkers whom God has placed in the years of my life.
Without the challenge and blessing of my encounters with these
folk, the idea and motivation for writing this book
would never have entered my mind.
God bless them every one.

I also dedicate this book to the
memory of C. S. Lewis, whose writing and
Christian example remain among the most powerful
influences in my life and a constant source of nourishment to
both sides of my brain. I've seen too much of life
to have any earthly heroes, but I may yet
make an exception in his case.

Contents

Editor's Foreword

Healthy Congregations

Christianity is a "first-person plural" religion, where communal worship, service, fellowship, and learning are indispensable for grounding and forming individual faith. The strength of Christianity in North America depends on the presence of healthy, spiritually nourishing, well-functioning congregations. Congregations are the cradle of Christian faith, the communities in which children of all ages are supported, encouraged, and formed for lives of service. Congregations are the habitat in which the practices of the Christian life can flourish.

As living organisms, congregations are by definition in a constant state of change. Whether the changes are in membership, pastoral leadership, lay leadership, the needs of the community, or the broader culture, a crucial mark of healthy congregations is their ability to deal creatively and positively with change. The fast pace of change in contemporary culture, with its bias toward, not against, change only makes the challenge of negotiating change all the more pressing for congregations.

Vital Worship

At the center of many discussions about change in churches today is the topic of worship. This is not surprising, for worship is at the center of congregational life. To "go to church" means, for most members of congregations, "to go to worship." In *How Do We Worship?*, Mark Chaves begins his analysis with the simple assertion, "Worship is the most central and public activity engaged in by American religious congregations" (Alban Institute, 1999, p. 1). Worship styles are one of the most significant reasons that people

choose to join a given congregation. Correspondingly, they are central to the identity of most congregations.

Worship is also central on a much deeper level. Worship is the locus of what several Christian traditions identify as the nourishing center of congregational life: preaching, common prayer, and the celebration of ordinances or sacraments. Significantly, what many traditions elevate to the status of "the means of grace" or even the "marks of the church" are essentially liturgical actions. Worship is central, most significantly, for theological reasons. Worship both reflects and shapes a community's faith. It expresses a congregation's view of God and enacts a congregation's relationship with God and each other.

We can identify several specific factors that contribute to spiritually vital worship and thereby strengthen congregational life.

- Congregations, and the leaders that serve them, need a shared vision for worship that is grounded in more than personal aesthetic tastes. This vision must draw on the deep theological resources of Scripture, the Christian tradition, and the unique history of the congregation.
- Congregational worship should be integrated with the whole life of the congregation. It can serve as the "source and summit" from which all the practices of the Christian life flow. Worship both reflects and shapes the life of the church in education, pastoral care, community service, fellowship, justice, hospitality, and every other aspect of church life.
- The best worship practices feature not only good worship "content," such as discerning sermons, honest prayers, creative artistic contributions, celebrative and meaningful rituals for baptism and the Lord's Supper. They also arise of out of good process, involving meaningful contributions from participants, thoughtful leadership, honest evaluation, and healthy communication among leaders.

Vital Worship, Healthy Congregations Series

The Vital Worship, Healthy Congregations Series is designed to reflect the kind of vibrant, creative energy and patient reflection

that will promote worship that is both relevant and profound. It is designed to invite congregations to rediscover a common vision for worship, to sense how worship is related to all aspects of congregational life, and to imagine better ways of preparing both better "content" and better "process" related to the worship life of their own congregations.

It is important to note that strengthening congregational life through worship renewal is a delicate and challenging task precisely because of the uniqueness of each congregation. This book series is not designed to represent a single denomination, Christian tradition, or type of congregation. Nor is it designed to serve as arbiter of theological disputes about worship. Books in the series will note the significance of theological claims about worship, but they may, in fact, represent quite different theological visions from each other, or from our work at the Calvin Institute of Christian Worship. That is, the series is designed to call attention to instructive examples of congregational life and to explore these examples in ways that allow readers in very different communities to compare and contrast these examples with their own practice. The models described in any given book may for some readers be instructive as examples to follow. For others, a given example may remind them of something they are already doing well, or something they will choose not to follow because of theological commitments or community history.

In the first volume in our series, *One Bread, One Body: Exploring Cultural Diversity in Worship*, Michael Hawn posed the poignant question "is there room for my neighbor at the table?" and explored what four multicultural congregations have to teach us about hospitality and the virtues of cross-cultural worship. His work helps us step back and reflect on the core identity of our congregations.

In our second volume, *Designing Worship Together: Models and Strategies for Worship Planning*, Norma deWaal Malefyt and Howard Vanderwell enter the trenches of weekly congregational life. They give us helpful insights into the process of how services are planned and led. It is hard to overstate the significance of this topic. For without a thoughtful, discerning, collaborative worship planning process, all manner of worship books, conferences, and renewal programs are likely either to make no inroads into the life

of a given congregation or, when they do, to damage rather than renew congregational life.

In the third volume, *When God Speaks through Change: Preaching in Times of Congregational Transition,* Craig Satterlee addresses the question of how worship (and particularly preaching) might best respond to times of significant congregational transition. The vast majority of published perspectives and resources for preaching and worship unwittingly assume a level of constancy in congregational life, taking for granted that the congregation will have the resources (emotional and otherwise) to absorb some significant new message or practice. However, on any given Sunday, a strikingly large number of churches are simply trying to cope with a significant transition in community life or leadership. These transitions do limit what preachers and worship leaders can do on Sunday, but they also present unparalleled opportunities for the reception of the gospel. For congregations in transition, this book provides a useful and necessary frame for viewing almost all other advice and resources about what should happen in public worship.

In the fourth volume, *Where 20 or 30 Are Gathered: Leading Worship in the Small Church,* Peter Bush and Christine O'Reilly probe a topic that is instructive not only for small congregations, but also for large ones. When representatives of small congregations attend worship conferences or read books about worship they are frequently confronted with practices and resources that are entirely impractical for their purposes, requiring time and money that simply aren't available. Yet, as Bush and O'Reilly demonstrate, "small" certainly does not mean "deficient." In fact, smaller congregations have the potential to achieve participation, flexibility, and intimacy that larger congregations find much harder to achieve. In the upside-down world of the kingdom of God, could it be that those of us from larger congregations should be attending conferences in smaller congregations, rather than just the other way around?

In this fifth volume, *With All Thy Mind,* Robert Glick turns our attention to the people who gather for worship. As alert pastors know so well, when worshipers assemble they bring with them remarkable differences in aptitude, temperament, and preferences. For leaders who eagerly desire that their congregations participate

in worship in knowing and engaged ways, coming to terms with this diversity is essential. It is otherwise too tempting for preachers to prepare sermons and musicians to prepare music for people who are just like themselves. Recent writers have given us several ways to understand the diversity of persons who worship: personality type indicators, theories of multiple intelligences, and right-brain/left-brain differences. Glick works with the latter approach to help us understand that some differences among us can't be resolved by simply asserting our own point of view more loudly. In contrast, there is much to be gained by discovering how differences in how we are wired can enrich our appreciation and love for each other. As Glick himself warns, readers (of any of these theories) must not overreach: these approaches give us a window into human diversity but should never simplify our view of each other or be used to avoid conflict over matters of significant pastoral concern. May Glick's readers find themselves with renewed commitments to attending to fellow worshipers and to various Christian traditions in discerning and pastorally sensitive ways.

By promoting encounters with instructive examples from various parts of the body of Christ, we pray that these volumes will help leaders make good judgments about worship in their congregations and that, by the power of God's Spirit, these congregations will flourish.

John D. Witvliet
Calvin Institute of Christian Worship

Foreword

When I was asked to write the foreword to Robert Glick's *With All Thy Mind,* I agreed to do so enthusiastically because of my friendship with Robert and my respect for his work.

Yet, I must admit that there was a reluctance in my soul to write this. My reluctance derived not from anything personal, but from the overabundance of books on worship. "What more can be said?" I thought to myself. And, then, another thought came into my mind: "So many books written on worship reflect a writer's personal preferences without any reference to the biblical story from which worship derives or integration with the way worship has been handed down throughout the history of the church." Many of the books on worship are either gimmicky or laden with a sentimental romantic notion of our relationship to God. So, yes, I picked up *With All Thy Mind* with some built-in apprehension, but knowing Robert, with a sense of expectancy as well.

Thanks be to God! Robert is a writer who is completely sensitive to the culture in which we live, conversant with the biblical roots of worship in God's story, well aware of the various historical traditions of worship, and, as if that is not enough, *With All Thy Mind* carries us into a deeper grasp of the explosion of the new worship awakening.

Glick understands the confusion about worship that has touched nearly every church in North America, Europe, South America, Asia, and Africa. Two worship renewals have been occurring simultaneously. First, the liturgical renewal sprang forth from the preparation for *The Constitution on the Sacred Liturgy,* the first document of Vatican II, published in 1963. This constitution called Catholics back to ancient ways of worship and resulted in not only

a reform among Catholics, but also a renewal that spread to many mainline Protestant churches and attracted a minority of evangelicals as well. Then in the late 1960s and early '70s, the Jesus People phenomena resulted in the birth of the chorus movement and eventually the spread of contemporary worship around the globe. These two movements were brought together in what became known as blended or convergence worship. In one way or another, almost every congregation in the world has been touched by one or the other of the movements.

In the meantime, culture has been moving at a rapid pace beneath all these movements, and these cultural movements cannot and have not been ignored by the church and worship renewal. The church bumps up against culture, and as it has been the case in recent years, defines itself in relationship to culture. Some churches and their worship have been defined *over against* culture. Other churches have accommodated themselves to culture, adapting worship to styles and sounds common to the culture in which people are immersed. Now culture is changing again. We realize that we live in a postmodern world where Christianity, once privileged, is now under attack. The post-9/11 world where terrorists threaten Christianity with a new religious and political domination forces us to ask once again "What is Christianity?" and "What is the worship that Christians do?"

Glick approaches this question by asking us to return to the scriptures, not as a set of propositions that can be used like building blocks to set forth a *case* to defend the Christian faith, but as a story that reveals God's activity in the world. And here, of course, is where we must go. We cannot build worship on current culture, nor can we build worship on what *we* think it ought to be. We must be radical and return to the root. The root from which worship springs is God's activity in history. Worship is all about God becoming involved in history, entering history through words, sign, and symbols of his presence in the world. The greatest of all signs is the real, actual presence of God in time, space, and history, when by the power of the Spirit, God became one of us in Jesus Christ "for us and our salvation," as the ancient creeds declare. Worship does this story. It sings it, proclaims it, enacts it in word and sign.

Glick also takes us into history to show us how we now live in not only a postmodern but also a post-denominational world. If you look back at the origin of every denomination, it becomes clear that each one was birthed in a renewal expressed in worship. Today, as we come into our new post-denominational era, it is imperative that we rediscover what is common to all of us—the story of God, which we do in worship.

And here is where Glick opens some new vistas of understanding for us. His understanding and application of how the brain functions speaks to the current renewal of sign and symbol in worship. God has wired our brains to be both rational and intuitive, concrete and imaginative, analytical and sympathetic, linear and holistic, segmented and pictorial, abstract and analogical, objective and subjective, literal and metaphoric, verbal and visual.

So then, the new worship awakening is about understanding our culture, rooting worship in scripture, realizing the need to be post-denominational, and affirming that worship engages the whole person. Thank you, Robert Glick. You spoke against my prejudices and fears, you touched my mind, my heart, and my will. May God bless *With All Thy Mind* and those who read it.

Robert Webber
Myers Professor of Ministry, Northern Seminary, Illinois
President, Institute for Worship Studies, Florida

Introduction

"Words, words, words . . . !" That's what I overheard a female student sigh to no one in particular as everyone filed out of the seminary chapel service. I wish now that I had asked her exactly what she meant by that. Was she referring to the chapel service alone? Or was she thinking as well of the three-hour class she had attended before the chapel service began? Maybe it was a reaction to her entire seminary experience. Whatever it was, it seemed to have been the chapel worship service that put her over the edge.

We have come a long way in the "worship wars" since all the upheavals began in the 1960s. Yet surprisingly, in many places worship still goes on pretty much as it did in 1950—same hymns, same order of worship, same feel. While some churches have changed their worship order and style many times, others give no indication that any sort of worship renewal has been going on over the past half century. So the foment goes on, the reactions and counterreactions, the new worship movements and philosophies, and, of course, the books! Who can keep up with the plethora of books on worship that steadily stream forth from a host of publishers large and small?

The worship terrain *has* changed a great deal! But all the books, experimentation, revision, and diversity of the past 50 years have yet to produce consensus even about what worship *is*, let alone *how* we should worship. Most denominational leaders do seem to understand now that worship is primarily about God and not about us and our needs. But we seem still to disagree about how this insight plays out in a worship service. We seem largely to have understood that the sacraments need to have a more central place than they used to, but few have gotten back to the pattern of

weekly communion modeled by the primitive church and urged by
the vast majority of the great historic reformers. We hear cries on
all fronts that worship must be culturally relevant. But the cultural
topography is changing under our feet at an ever-accelerating rate.
To which segment of the population shall we be relevant—builders, boomers, busters, or the emerging 20-something set? And shall
our services of worship be relevant to nonchurched seekers or to
seasoned saints—or to both, if that is possible? As the racial and
ethnic ratios of the American population continue to shift, these
factors further complicate issues of relevance in Christian worship.

I see no real consensus yet. Contemporary worship styles are
certainly becoming more common, perhaps even the norm in some
parts of the country. Yet, in the South at least, it is still quite easy to
find just about any style of worship one would like within any of
the mainline denominations, and beyond. Perhaps it is a good thing
that one need not leave his or her own theological tradition to find
a style of worship that suits. But many have a growing concern that
various members of a family may find themselves attending different churches, or at least different services within a given church,
for all to find the worship style that "meets their needs" (a phrase
that warrants more critical examination). Others voice concern that
it is increasingly hard to discern the unity or universality of Christ's
church amid such a diversity of worship styles.

Perhaps this current state of affairs is precisely what we should
expect. One cannot expect calm waters during a hurricane. While
it will be the work of later generations to interpret and to provide
labels for the religious events of the past five decades or so, it seems
clear that a reformation of corporate Christian worship will be a
major feature, if not the defining feature, of this era of church history. Few would disagree that we are in a sea of change. Anyone
who remembers the placid world of corporate worship prior to
1965 or so knows this well enough. It remains to be seen whether
this era will be referred to as a "twentieth-century worship renewal"
or a full-fledged "reformation of worship," but we are clearly in
the midst of something huge. And we are merely in the "midst" of
it. What is happening may finally be thought of, if the Lord tarries,
as a twenty-first century phenomenon, for the pace of worship reform seems only to be quickening. If worship writer Robert Webber
is anywhere near accurate in his appraisal of the 20-something age

segment of the church, we are just now beginning to see some of the most profound adjustments to worship style and theology as this age group begins increasingly to exert its unique influence.[1]

At this point, somewhere in the middle of the storm, I am beginning to see bits and pieces coming together of what may be a highly significant aspect of this modern worship reformation. More and more people are addressing the importance of nonverbal forms of communication in corporate worship. That is to be expected, since intuitive, emotive, sensual ways of knowing are a definitive part of the current postmodern era. But at least one other factor accounts for this growing attention to nonverbal communication. A new interest in early-church worship patterns has been an influential element in some branches of current worship renewal. As one looks far back into the church's past, as many are doing these days, back before American frontier revivalism, before the Enlightenment, before either the Reformation or the Middle Ages, one sees a church that was surprisingly well integrated between the logical and the intuitive, the intellectual and the emotional, the verbal and the symbolic. Early Christian writers such as Justin Martyr describe worship services in which the Lord's Supper as well as a sermon was offered each week. The weekly celebration of the sacraments cannot help but infuse emotional and symbolic elements into worship. This practice, in and of itself, would make worship in the early church significantly different from much Protestant worship. Further, hymns surviving from the early church are often rich in symbolic imagery. Sun and light, winter and spring are used as metaphors for God and the Christian life. The hymns often abound with imaginative and pictorial allusions to biblical scenes and personalities. And even the allegorical style of biblical interpretation so common in the early church requires the mind to think symbolically.

Today's younger people, born and bred in a postmodernist world, are hungry not just to know *about* God, but actually to *know* and *experience* God with all that they are—mind, heart, body, and soul. Thus, they are increasingly attracted to worship services that are rich in nonverbal as well as verbal elements.

Some denominational and theological groups have traditionally focused on the centrality of the spoken word, crafting a sermon-dominated worship style based on logical sequences of thought.

Others have focused on more experiential worship, centering on worshipers *feeling* the presence of God. Often each group sees its worship style as a necessary corrective to the inadequacies of the other, thus fostering skepticism toward other worship traditions. As a result, both groups, fearful of the excesses of the other, fail to achieve a healthy balance.

I write as an ordained minister of Word and Sacrament in the Presbyterian Church (U.S.A.). I write also as a college and seminary professor of worship and church music. The institution where I have taught and worshiped since 1988 is the college and seminary of another Reformed denomination—the Associate Reformed Presbyterian Church. This seminary is noted for having a multi-denominational student body. Thus, my association with Erskine College and Seminary has profoundly enriched my understanding, not only of the larger Reformed family but of worship traditions internationally.

I am a professional organist and choral director who has given over 40 years of professional musical service to the church of Jesus Christ, having started my first job as a paid organist at the tender age of 13. Although my musical tastes are quite varied, my decided preference is for more complex or classical forms of artistic expression. This is true of all art forms, liturgy, and even cuisine. All these factors color my perceptions of what is going on in worship, and it is just as well that I confess them from the start.

I am Presbyterian by choice, but my debt to other denominations is incalculable. I was baptized and raised in the Methodist tradition, and I owe my home congregation eternal thanks for a childhood and youth filled to overflowing with the truths of Scripture and countless examples of rock-solid faith and love for Jesus. It was this congregation as well that nurtured and encouraged my budding musical leadership skills. In time, I went on to serve as an organist for congregations in the United Church of Christ, the Evangelical Lutheran Church in America, the Episcopal Church, and of course the Presbyterian Church (U.S.A.). In addition, I have often substituted as organist in the Roman Catholic Church, various Baptist churches, and many independent congregations. To many of these I am indebted for awakening my deep love of the ancient liturgy of the church and for instilling in me a sense of the impor-

tance and godliness of aesthetics in worship. To others I owe thanks for teaching me the value of well-considered words fitly read or spoken. To all I am thankful for opening my eyes to the breadth of styles of preaching and the revelation that the Word of God can and does proceed through many sermonic styles.

Through the many years of serving in all these denominations, I was doing more than merely learning a new order of worship or even a new tradition. I was learning to know the *people*. I learned that hanging around with a Presbyterian crowd was a different sort of cultural experience from being with a bunch of Episcopalians. Folk differed. Each group had a different ethos that went far beyond worship style. One could sense it in the choir room, the committee meeting, or the banquet hall. As I think back over all the congregations I have served, a unique feel characterized each denominational tradition.

I see a growing awareness, especially among the young, that worship must engage the whole person, and I believe that this is a healthy trend. And this trend comes at a time when phenomenal progress is being made in the field of brain science. We are learning more every day about the locations within the human brain that control specific ways of knowing and communicating. This new knowledge is having a profound impact not only in the fields of neurology and psychology, but in educational fields as well. In this book, we'll explore how what we're learning about the brain has deep ramifications also for Christian worship. We'll explore the interrelationships between what we know about the divinely instituted worship life of ancient Israel, the greater biblical witness regarding worship, our various denominational worship traditions, and what we now know about the complex working relationships among the various thought centers of the human brain. As we explore these rather complex interconnections, my hope is that churches of all sorts might be moved to reexamine their worship traditions in light of the newly revealed wonders of our God-given brains, and that in so doing, we may all be led to worship that is fuller, richer, more biblical, and thus more receptive to the Holy Spirit of God. For the Spirit of God is most certainly creating a new thing amid our stormy worship seas, and not all of our worship "boats" are equally equipped to weather the storm.

Questions for Thought and Discussion

Before moving into the text of the book, take some time to reflect on your particular experiences in worship. Be creative in answering these questions. If you find that you are not a thinker "in words," devise another means to respond.[2]

1. Journal or discuss with a group the various worship styles you have experienced throughout your life. Think through both the positive and negative ways in which you have responded.

2. Think of various modes of music (classical, rock 'n roll, hip hop, rap, jazz, blues, other forms). Reflect on those that have proved uplifting, encouraging, life-giving, comforting, or inspiring to you. Reflect on other modes that have irritated, frustrated, confused, or saddened you.

3. The text details the use of both verbal (spoken word, intellectual, and logical) and nonverbal (intuitive, emotional, and symbolic) forms of communication in corporate worship. Define from your past worship experiences elements of worship that evoked intellectual, logical, and verbal responses from you and aspects that evoked more intuitive, emotional, and symbolic responses. What elements of worship have been particularly meaningful in aiding you to *know* and *experience* God?

Chapter One

The Human Brain

I praise you because I am fearfully and wonderfully made.
—Psalm 139:14

The intuitive mind is a sacred gift and the rational mind is a faithful servant. We have created a society that honors the servant and has forgotten the gift.
—Albert Einstein

It was a 90-minute philosophy class. The professor had been lecturing for at least the past 60 minutes about Platonic thought. I had reached the saturation point. It was not that I was bored—quite the opposite: I really wanted to understand. I simply could not follow the complexities of the logic. Finally, at just about the time I had reached exhaustion, he began to draw a diagram on the chalkboard. It was like the reappearance of the sun after long days of rain. I suddenly understood! I learned more in the next five minutes than I had in the previous 60. As the semester went on, this professor often saved the day by the timely addition of a visual illustration. The teacher in me made a note about the power of visual aids.

The next semester, I again found myself in a class in which a professor was well into a lengthy exposition of a particular point of theology. It occurred to me that the study of theology made mental demands similar to the study of philosophy. And once again, I was near mental exhaustion. I had vivid memories of my feeling from the previous year, but this time no visual aids seemed to be forthcoming. Finally I raised my hand. "I'm having a hard time grasping the concept here. Is there a way you can make a diagram of this on the board?" My request seemed to perplex the professor. He looked pained for a few moments and finally found a way to represent the

concept with a few simple sketches to illustrate his points. Feeble as these attempts were, I once again found them helpful. But as this semester progressed, the professor seldom used the board, except to write more words.

This tale of two teachers illustrates some of the issues related to the ways the human brain takes in and transmits information. The first professor was naturally inclined to combine verbal and non-verbal communication in his teaching. The second relied almost exclusively on the spoken word. The mere suggestion that he present a concept visually seemed truly to tax his imagination. The first showed a marked use of both right and left lobes of the cerebral cortex of the brain. The second showed a communication style that relied more on centers in the left lobe. This illustration also shows that I, too, have a significant amount of right-brain specialization. Information I receive in an exclusively verbal format fails to communicate as effectively as that combined with nonverbal data.

An exploration of the basic structures of the brain will aid us in understanding how these different parts of the brain process information.

The Cerebral Cortex

The human brain is divided into three main sections. The archipallium and limbic brain sustain basic life functions and other functions humans hold in common with other animals, such as bonding instincts, memory skills, and primal emotions. These inner sections of the brain are virtually surrounded by the cerebral cortex, which constitutes five-sixths of the brain's total mass. The cerebral cortex is common to all mammals but is most highly developed in humans.

This part of the brain controls functions of language, logic, self-awareness, aesthetics, and creative thought in general. The cerebral cortex is divided into right and left lobes, or hemispheres, each approximately the size of an adult human fist. This part of the brain is also called the cerebrum; its two lobes are the cerebral hemispheres.

Connecting these two hemispheres are a number of bundles of nerve fibers called commissures, the largest of which is the corpus callosum. It is through these bundles, these "bridges" of neurons, that information passes from one hemisphere of the cerebral cortex to the other.

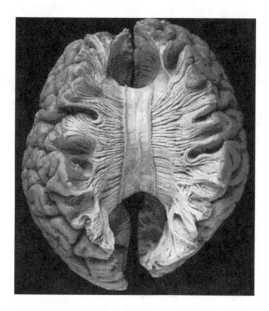

Figure I. Photo of a human brain showing the corpus callosum dividing the two cerebral hemispheres.[1]

So when we speak of the right or left brain, we do not mean the entire brain. We are referring to one of these two outer hemispheres, each one specializing in different thought processes. The left hemisphere is the primary location for the "three Rs"—reading, writing, and arithmetic; logic or reason; and most matters of analysis. It tends to think in abstract, segmental, sequential lines of thought.

The right hemisphere is the primary location for visual imagery, spatial dimensions, movement, music appreciation, and aesthetic apprehension in general. It tends to see things in concrete, holistic terms, creating a synthesis of the bits of data it receives—seeing the forest rather than the trees. Right-brain thinking tends to be intuitive rather than rational.

Notice that each is the *primary* location for these various ways of thinking. A common misunderstanding, especially in the more popular applications of this theory, is to oversimplify these differences, assuming that each hemisphere operates pretty much independently of the other. Such assumptions are grossly misleading. There is a constant interchange of data between the hemispheres through the commissures, such that very few mental processes could be said to come from one side only. In fact, human thought is so complex that almost any thought process will engage multiple sections of both sides of the brain. Still, scientists have isolated particular portions of the brain as centers for specific kinds of thought—at least for most people.

MENTAL ACTIVITY	LEFT HEMISPHERE	RIGHT HEMISPHERE
Processing Data	Logical/Rational	Intuitive
	Concrete	Uses Imagination
	Analytical/Detail oriented	Sees whole picture and synthesizes
	Sequential/Linear	Holistic
	Segmental	Pictorial
	Abstract	Sees analogies, resemblances
	Objective	Subjective
	Literal	Metaphoric
	Focuses on facts	Focuses on the *meaning* of facts
Specialized Functions	Verbal (reading, writing, etc.)	Visual
	Arithmetic/Mathematics	Musical appreciation
	Awareness of time	Aesthetics
	Planning and strategizing	Geometry
		Spatial relationships
		Symbolism
		Emotions

Figure 2. Characteristics of the Right and Left Hemispheres of the Human Brain

A Brief History of Split-Brain Research

More widespread interest in the two hemispheres of the brain grew out of experiments done by Roger W. Sperry and Ronald Meyers in the 1950s and 1960s at the California Institute of Technology in Pasadena. Sperry's research in this area led to his being awarded the 1981 Nobel Prize in Physiology or Medicine "for his discoveries concerning the functional specialization of the cerebral hemispheres."[2]

Sperry and Meyers discovered that by severing the corpus callosum, the bundle of fibers connecting the right and left cerebral hemispheres, significant relief could be given to epileptic patients who were not responding to anti-epileptic drugs. The results were immediate and amazing, though controversial. Scientists had known that partially cutting portions of the brain had an effect on seizures and that the corpus callosum was somehow involved with epilepsy. But the proposal to sever these fibers entirely was breathtaking! Early tests on cats and monkeys were quite successful, though, and in 1961 doctors finally fully severed the corpus callosum in a severely epileptic human being, in an effort to relieve the seizures. The operations seemed at first to have little ill effect. The patients seemed completely normal. But before long these patients began to exhibit curious behaviors resulting from the operation. For example, they might hold a spoon in their left hand and not be able to say what it was, if they could not see it. Yet if the spoon was transferred to the right hand, the patient could immediately say the word "spoon."

A flurry of testing and experimentation was initiated by Sperry and his colleagues, resulting in a vast increase in our understanding of the relationships between the right and left brains. In one common category of experiments, patients would use an apparatus that projected images to each eye separately from the other eye. (Information received through the right eye is sent to the left hemisphere of the brain, and vice versa.[3]) If an image, such as a spoon, was projected to the right eye only, the left side of the brain would be engaged. In such cases, the patients would be able to *say* that the object was a spoon. But if the spoon was projected to the *left* eye, the silent *right* side of the brain would be engaged. Now the patients

would *say* they saw nothing at all. Yet, using only their *left* hand, they would be able to correctly pick out a spoon from among a group of objects, even though they just said they saw nothing. In fact patients would not be able to say what was held in their left hand even while holding it! The connection between the two hemispheres had been cut; communication between the two had been radically limited.

In another category of experiments, patients would be blindfolded and have some object placed in their left hand. The object could not be verbally identified, but patients could act out how the object might be used. If asked to describe what they were acting out, they would not be able to verbalize what they were doing, though they would know they were doing *something*. When the object was moved to the right hand, the left side of the brain was engaged and immediately patients were able to say what the object was.

Such experiments performed on people whose cerebral hemispheres are forced to act independently of each other reveal much about the unique characteristics of each hemisphere. For some time the right hemisphere was believed to be inferior because it is nonverbal. It didn't seem to "know" very much. Michael Gazzaniga, who was part of the Cal Tech team working with Sperry, tried to discover the true potential of the right brain. Ten objects were placed behind a screen. Split-brain patients were asked to reach underneath the screen and feel the objects. Meanwhile an image of one of the objects was projected to the left eye only, thus engaging the right side of the brain. The patients were immediately able through touch alone to find an object that corresponded with the projected image. Even when the test was made more difficult by not providing the exact images projected, patients were able to choose correctly the objects that were related to the projected image. For example, an image of a cigarette was projected to the left eye and the patient chose an ashtray among the felt objects, when no cigarette was present. Such experiments established that right brain is no dummy. It may be illiterate and mute, but it is imaginative, creative, and quick.[4]

These findings received a great deal of publicity and in time entered into the vocabulary of the general public. It is not uncommon to hear someone claim to be a right-brained or left-brained person. People who were prone to express themselves through a

linear stream of logic were said to be left-brain dominant; someone who relied on intuition rather than logical reasoning was said to be right-brain dominant. Dominance, in fact, became the more-or-less standard way to speak of patterns of thought that seemed consistently to prefer one hemisphere over the other.

Hemispheric Dominance

Even a cursory observation of human activity will reveal that some people naturally seem to use modes of thought that more often come from the left brain. Others naturally gravitate to right-brained thought patterns. Some use both lobes more or less equally. People seem to exhibit brain dominance over the entire gamut from extreme right-brainedness to extreme left, and every combination in between.

But this is not to say that we *cannot* consciously choose to engage one side over the other. Mathematics is a largely left-brained endeavor. Left-brain-dominant people normally should do better at it than right-brained people. This, however, does not prohibit right-brained people from exercising their left side, or from getting better at it. However, it will take more effort—and for some much more! And their success may still be limited.

Hemispheric dominance provides a way of describing and understanding many of the obvious differences we see in each other every day. One need only read the list of characteristics in figure 2 on page 10, and certain individuals will likely come immediately to mind, and we will at least compare these characteristics to what we know about ourselves from a lifetime of experiences. As a musician, I cannot avoid noticing that music appreciation is a right-brained function. I see mathematics as an attribute of the left hemisphere, and I immediately remember the low grades in mathematics that followed me throughout my public school career. I begin to assume that I must be right-brain dominant. But then I notice that I am more of a logical, sequential thinker than an intuitive one. Sorting out facts is central to how I think and what I value. So I see some significant left-brained traits in myself as well. Thus, I realize that one cannot be too hasty or simplistic in ascertaining natural hemispheric preferences.

Of course, the ramifications of Sperry's work for the various fields of teaching and learning were obvious and there was no dearth of research and writing on the subject. As word of left-brain/right-brain theory reached a more general audience, pop psychologists began to disseminate exaggerated versions of the theory, at times building whole philosophies or belief systems around these exaggerations. The two basic errors, generally, were to assume that the right and left hemispheres controlled rigidly opposite functions and that each operated pretty much independently of the other. As one can see from figure 2, there is indeed a great deal of "oppositeness" about the dual lists of characteristics. If the left lobe is objective, the right is subjective. If the left is rational, the right is imaginative. But a closer look at the lists reveals a great deal more subtlety than that. Some characteristics have no exact opposites. What is the opposite of aesthetics? What is the opposite of mathematics? What is the opposite of visual imagery? One can see that any view of this subject that discounts the profound interrelatedness of the two spheres is doomed from the onset. The left hemisphere can tell you that many rows of roses are displayed at the flower shop, but it needs the right brain to tell you which colors are available. The right hemisphere may be enjoying a piece of music, but it is the analytical left hemisphere that can tell you that what you are listening to is rhythm and blues. In fact, both sides of the brain are involved to one degree or another in nearly every thought process. Sperry's original findings have been greatly refined and modified as further studies have been conducted, revealing a much greater complexity than originally observed.

The Triune Brain

We have seen that the two hemispheres of the cerebral cortex make up most of the total mass of the brain. The remaining portion is composed of two other general sections, the archipallium and the limbic brain. These three sections make up our total brain—a triune structure. The archipallium grows directly out of the spinal column and includes the brain stem, medulla, pons, cerebellum, and olfactory bulbs. This portion of the brain controls most of our au-

tomatic or instinctual functions, such as survival and physical maintenance of organs, mating, aggression/defense mechanisms, and smell.

The middle brain, the limbic brain, wraps itself around the archipallium. Some of the functions of the limbic brain are similar to the those of the archipallium. More to our interests in this book, this portion of the brain controls memories of life experiences and emotional reactions related to attachment and survival, such as a mother's instinct to protect her young or anyone's instinct to take whatever steps are necessary not to starve. With these functions of the limbic brain, we can begin to see some connections to religion. Scripture speaks of the parent's bonds to a child as similar to God's attachment to us. Or, perhaps, a fiery sermon on the dangers of hell might trigger the survival emotion of fear in a listener. But while these functions might be given a religious connection, the true seat of religious thought is the cortex, and we shall limit our investigation to the cortex for the remainder of the book.

Continuing Research

Research on the human brain continues at an intense level. Theories about how the brain actually works come and go with amazing speed. Some scientists believe that the triune brain theory, recent as it is, is already outdated. The rapid rate at which succeeding brain theories are developed and dismissed should serve as a warning for us not to draw many hard-and-fast conclusions about exactly how the brain works.

In fact, fewer and fewer experts are willing to speak of left- or right-brain dominance at all. Indeed, as is so often the case in any field, the more experts discover, the less they seem to know for sure. The complexities of the brain are eye-crossing. It is not so much that Sperry's work is being rejected as that it is being continually refined. Dale Purves, director of the Center for Cognitive Neuroscience at Duke University, confirms:

> Sperry's work is impeccable, and a remarkable achievement. He confirmed the findings of clinical neurologists during the 100 or so years preceding the 1960s, who surmised that the left and right

brains have overlapping but significantly different functions in a number of respects. Recent work with non-invasive imaging have confirmed Sperry's observations and extended what he found.[5]

But with an influx of data showing the complexities involved, Sperry's basic right/left dichotomy is now generally believed to be too simplistic. For example, we now know that both sides of the brain do visual/spatial tasks. And music, often considered a right-brain entity, actually calls into action many portions of the brain—both right and left. Rhythmic apprehension occurs in the left hemisphere, timbre (tone color) in the right. Harmonic analysis occurs in the left, general enjoyment or appreciation of that harmony in the right.

Other factors further cloud the picture. Sequential, logical thinking had been considered a left-brain trait. But George Ringholz, assistant professor of neurology at the Emory School of Medicine, points out:

> Gender and handedness are also important factors to account for. Women tend to have a higher number of inter-hemispheric connections than men, and therefore, their communication typically is more multi-modal. It is probably more accurate to describe sequential, logical communicators as having a "left hemisphere *style*" of communication [rather than left hemisphere *dominance*].[6]

Purves agrees that replacement of the word "dominant" with the word "style" is probably helpful: "The idea of dominance is misleading, since the left and right hemispheres simply do different things." But don't some people have a tendency to favor one type of thought over another? And might not this inclination amount to a sort of dominance of one hemisphere over the other, at least for certain kinds of thought? For most experts the answer is, "We simply don't know yet." As Purves summarizes, "These differences certainly exist and they are clearly innate, but the neural bases are not well understood, and a good deal of caution is therefore in order. . . . Neuroscientists know a lot less about these issues than you may think."

Both Purves and Ringholz agree that specific locations in the cerebral cortex specialize in certain kinds of thought and that many thought processes are unique to each hemisphere. Yet they urge caution and hesitate to draw many conclusions. One can easily understand the reticence these experts exhibit in stating what is known for sure. They are scientists. Everything in their training warns them to test and retest any hypothesis before accepting it as fact. The more they work with matters of cerebral lateralization,[7] the more complexity they find. Even though it is becoming ever clearer that the right and left hemispheres of the cerebral cortex do perform specialized cognitive tasks, and even though many people clearly seem to prefer using certain parts of the brain over others, experts simply will not endorse reducing this evidence to assertions of mere right- or left-brain dominance. They are finding that a great many cognitive tasks involve both sides of the brain, and too many issues such as handedness, gender, and personality have yet to be sorted out. They need to explore as well why, for a small minority of people, the thought centers for a given task are not located where they are for most other people.

For scientists, too many unresolved issues remain for them to commit to definitive statements of how the two hemispheres interrelate. Yet there is consistent agreement among them about the basic premise of this book—people do exhibit styles of thought that tend to prefer certain locations of the brain over others. And for many, this tendency amounts to a preference for one hemisphere over the other.

The Cerebral Hemispheres and Holistic Worship

We are fearfully and wonderfully made! Our interest in this book is to explore how what we are learning about the human brain might provide insight into how Christians worship. We have seen that the brain is radically complex but a masterpiece of organization. It is a micromanager par excellence with a specialized location for every aspect of every cognitive process.

We have seen that the language of right- or left-brain dominance, still so common in pop psychology and in the population at
large, is inadequate to describe the complexities of the human
thought process. It is not that such language has been proved to be
incorrect; it is merely too simplistic.

We know that different people seem to prefer thought processes
that use certain parts of the brain more than others. Some people
are more logical and others more intuitive, for example. Others
seem to move from logical to intuitive thinking with relative ease.
Some people are aural learners, and others are visual learners. These
things we know from experience. And now we know that each of
these thought patterns emanates from a location in the brain—better, a series of locations—that specialize in these ways of thinking.
If we can no longer speak of right- and left-brain dominance, we
can still affirm that different people use different parts of their brains
to varying degrees, and that these differences have considerable
ramifications for Christian worship. Christian worship often tends
to focus on words—a custom that suits some people but not others. Those who are comfortable with a wordy worship experience
should consider the consequences of not worshiping with the whole
self. Those who are less able to process large amounts of verbiage
successfully may do better in less word-oriented worship traditions,
assuming that their life situations allow for this choice, or they may
simply need to rise to the challenge of developing their facility with
a less comfortable style of learning.

In this book, we will consider what it might mean to engage
our brains in worship more *holistically*. Yet, as I have tried to demonstrate, there is no reason to abandon all talk of right- or left-
brain ways of knowing or communicating. So while I will avoid
talk of cerebral dominance, I believe it is appropriate and accurate
to affirm that certain types of thought and communication emanate primarily from the right or left side of the brain. I will proceed
on that assumption.

Our study of the human brain lends new insight to Jesus's words,
"You shall love the Lord your God with all your heart, and with all
your soul, and with all your mind" (Matt. 22:37). What qualities
would characterize a worship service that enabled us to engage
God through as many parts of our brains as possible, or that simi-

larly enabled God to engage us as whole people? Could our failure to do so be a means by which we unwittingly quench the Holy Spirit? What can we assume about God's intentions for our worship, from what we know about the way our brains have been created? How holistic in this sense are the descriptions of worship found in the Old and New Testaments of Holy Scripture? Do some Christian traditions or denominations achieve holistic worship better than others? What impact does culture have on such matters? These are some of the issues we will explore in the following chapters. It is a fascinating study, one that reminds us over and over that we are indeed fearfully and wonderfully made.

Questions for Thought and Discussion

1. Spend a few minutes meditating on Matthew 22:37. What does Jesus mean by "heart, soul, and mind"?
2. Reflecting on your classroom experiences, list in two columns specific learning skills and experiences that were easy for you and those that were difficult. Compare your columns with figure 2. Are there parallels between your two columns and those in figure 2 that help you to understand how you think or process information?
3. Spend a few minutes meditating on Psalm 139:13–15. God has created each human being "in his image and likeness." Describe who you are as God's design.
4. Think about worship experiences from your past. Again listing in two columns, think through aspects of worship that were both comfortable and uncomfortable for you. Compare your list with figure 2. Are there any parallels between figure 2 and your list that help you understand your worship preferences?

Chapter Two

Historical Survey of Holistic Brain Issues

*I will pray with my spirit, but I will also pray with my
 mind;
I will sing with my spirit, but I will also sing with my
 mind.*

—1 Corinthians 14:15

*"Would not conversation be much more rational than danc-
ing?" said Jane Austen's Miss Bingley. "Much more rational," replied Mr. Bingley, "but much less like a ball."*
—C. S. Lewis, in his essay
"Myth Became Fact," quoting from Pride and Prejudice

It is tempting to react to whole brain theory as if it were something
new on the face of the earth, and in some ways it is. It is only
during the past 50 years that all the research described in chapter 1
took place. It is only recently that we have begun to understand
first the differences and then the relationships between these two
hemispheres.

But once we become more familiar with the attributes, the personalities, of the various portions of the brain, we begin to see that
theologians and philosophers have observed and written about these
various modes of thought for almost as long as people have been
thinking about thinking. This subject resonates more broadly and
commonly than just among the deep thinkers of a given age. We
can easily trace the dynamics, often the conflict, between these various ways of thinking at any point in history. Carol Doran, associate professor of church music at Colgate Rochester Divinity School,
and Thomas Troeger, professor of preaching at Iliff School of

Theology, speak of these dynamics in their joint effort *Trouble at the Table*:

> There have been periods in the church's history when certain senses and faculties were favored over others and were lifted up as the superior or only way to approach God in worship. We think especially of the reformers of the 16th century, who stressed the use of the ear as "the gate to heaven." If we have been raised in such a tradition and its history is precious to us, we may consider those reformers' statements to be the last and authoritative word on the subject. However, recent scholarship has helped us realize that the nearly exclusive emphasis upon "hearing God's word" needs to be examined in the light of the historical conditions that gave rise to such a view, especially the liturgical practices and decoration of the interior space of the churches in that period.[1]

I do not question the good intentions of these reformers. But could it be that at times our own zeal for biblical faithfulness to and doctrinal purity in worship issues is not entirely pristine? Might at least a slight bit of personal taste, our preference for using a certain part of the brain, be subconsciously drawing us to the theological or philosophical interpretation that resonates best with that style of thought? Honest Bible scholars and theologians have always known the dangers of eisegesis—of reading into a text the meaning we desperately want it to have. Modern brain research merely shows us a little more about why this is so easy to do. It's not always simply a matter of sin tainting our view. Our own God-given "hemisphere of choice" is always coloring our reactions and opinions. This natural preference for certain modes of thought is another reason why we in the greater church so desperately need each other. We are so likely to huddle together in our little camps of like-minded (like-brained?) believers.

But not everyone has the option of huddling together in purely homogenous units. Friction naturally arises as people react differently to any given worship issue. During the sixteenth-century Reformation, Ulrich Zwingli had the churches of Zurich "cleansed" of virtually all painting, statuary, and nonessential furnishings. He wrote, "In Zurich we have churches which are positively luminous;

the walls are beautifully white." A traveler passing through Zurich after these changes wrote of the city's main church, "There was nothing at all inside, and it was hideous."[2]

Let's explore some other examples in history where such duality has manifested itself.

Pythagoras versus Aristotle

In his insightful book *The Sacred in Music*, Albert Blackwell, professor of religion at Furman University, in Greenville, South Carolina, discusses the difference in thought between two ancient Greeks—Pythagoras and Aristotle. Pythagoras believed that the fundamental realities of the universe were structural and mathematical. These realities are all integrated into a single system.[3] Music, for example, was to be studied not by listening to it, but by analyzing the complex mathematical structure of the harmonic or overtone series. Plato seems to share Pythagoras' scorn of musicians who engage in the study of music by actually *listening* to it. He writes in his *Republic*:

> They talk of something they call minims and, laying their ears alongside, as if trying to catch a voice from next door, some affirm they can hear a note between and that this is the least interval and the unit of measurement, while others insist that the strings now render identical sounds, both preferring their ears to their minds.[4]

Aristotle and many others in his generation are cut from a different pattern. Compare the Plato quotation above with the following by Aristoxenus, a student of Aristotle:

> We endeavor to supply proofs that will be in agreement with the phenomena—in this unlike our predecessors. For some of these introduced extraneous reasoning, and rejecting the senses as inaccurate, fabricated rational principles, asserting that height and depth of pitch consist in certain numerical ratios and relative rates of vibration—a theory utterly extraneous to the subject and quite

at variance with the phenomena. . . . Our method rests in the last
resort on an appeal to the two faculties of hearing and intellect. . . .
We must in matters of harmony accustom both ear and intellect
to a correct judgment of the permanent and changeable element
alike.[5]

To one who has studied the characteristics of hemispheric specialties, it is easy to categorize these contrasting approaches.
Pythagoras and Plato speak of mathematics and analytical technique. They are at home in their left brain. Plato's description of
those who lay their ears "alongside [a plucked string] as if trying to
catch a voice from next door" reminds me of so many conversations I have had with people who have had little contact with or
interest in the musical world. It is as if they have literally no place
in their mind to even conceive of, let alone relate to, a musical
aesthetic experience. Plato seems to see little practical value in studying music by listening to it. One can easily detect his mocking tone
toward those who do.

How different is the more holistic approach of Aristoxenus!
He describes a purely mathematical approach as "fabricated principles" and "utterly extraneous to the subject." For him, it is pa-
tently obvious that the senses must also be involved in a study of
music. Here are the voices of two minds pretty much talking past
each other. It is doubtful that either would ever convince the other;
they are perceiving musical reality out of different parts of the brain.

Dura-Europos: To Paint or Not to Paint

Moving ahead to the early Christian era, we next see how the primitive church, at least in some settings, ministered to the whole brain.
In present-day Syria, along the banks of the Euphrates River, ar-
chaeologists have explored the ruins of the ancient village of Dura-
Europos. Among the ruins is the earliest Christian house church
yet to be discovered. Experts believe it was built in 232 B.C. and
that it served as a church from A.D. 240 until 256, when the city
was destroyed. This church, however, has survived to such a degree
that even the paintings on the walls are still largely intact. Of the

eight rooms in this church, the baptistry and assembly hall are the best preserved. Behind the font in the baptistry is a painting of the Good Shepherd and the sheep and another of the fall of Adam and Eve.

Biblical scenes portrayed on other walls include the procession of women to the tomb on Easter, the healing of the paralytic, Jesus walking on the water, the woman at the well, and David and Goliath. In other sites where early churches once stood, we find very early evidence that expensive communion ware and other implements were used in churches—all this prior to the time when Constantine legalized and started funding Christian worship.[6] The presence of fine art in these earliest places of worship raises the question of why these tiny, often struggling churches went to such trouble and expense just to have beautiful things around. One can imagine some of the elders complaining, "The money spent on these things should rather have been given to the poor." But the very presence of these objects in these primitive churches testifies to another way of understanding art and why art was valued in the early church by at least some Christians, then as now. True, some of these congregations may have installed these aesthetics just to keep up with the folks at the synagogue down the street.[7] But as we study the paintings in the baptistry of the house church at Duro-Europos, and the people who lived there, a deeper meaning begins to emerge.

The small community at Dura-Europos was under almost constant siege by Parthians, then Romans, and finally the Persians, who destroyed it in 256. Though Christianity was more than two centuries old by this time, it was still a religion struggling for its place in the world. Archeological finds in the community suggest that there were strong multicultural traditions comingling there. Janet Walton, associate professor of worship at Union Seminary in New York, points out:

> For the community at Dura, these subjects [of the wall paintings] described significant moments in the history of God's relationship with people, emphasizing a divine response to human beings in need. . . . They saw in this art an active expression of divine/human interaction applicable to their most critical and yet their most common concerns, providing images of courage, strength

and protection that spoke concretely to the present joys and sorrows of that community. . . . That members of this community chose art to aid them in their quest not only reflects the religious practice of the time but also their recognition of its value for them.[8]

More specifically, Walton suggests that these paintings stimulated the congregation's memory of God's power and his past response to human need (Jesus as the good shepherd, David and Goliath, Jesus walking on the water), challenged them to reconsider the demands of the Christian gospel (Adam and Eve, the women at the tomb, the woman at the well), served as a complement to rather than a competition with verbal expressions of worship, and finally, stimulated a variety of senses.

Don Campbell, professor of music at Naropa Institute in Boulder, Colorado, in his book *Introduction to the Musical Brain*, emphasizes the importance of this final point by repeating the following phrase numerous times throughout in bold capital letters: **THE MORE CONNECTIONS THAT CAN BE MADE IN THE BRAIN, THE MORE INTEGRATED THE EXPERIENCE IS WITHIN MEMORY.**[9]

The house church at Dura-Europos gives quiet testimony that at least some of its congregants understood this truth about worshiping holistically and were willing to act accordingly, perhaps at considerable expense.

The Confessions of St. Augustine: Words versus Music

Our next historical vignette takes us to the writing desk of that much-vexed saint, Augustine of Hippo. The Confessions of Augustine were written as an extended prayer, the entire work being addressed to God. At one point, the author is confessing his perplexity over the relationship between musical tunes and the sacred texts set to them. He is aware that the music often raises the impact of the text beyond what it might be without the music. Indeed, the music often creates in him a "contentment of the flesh" that subtly "runs ahead" of the meaning of the words and influences the mean-

ing of them. This to him is a sin, as we shall see. On the other hand, at times he fears he errs on the side of too much strictness in these matters. Then he remembers how Athanasius used to make those who chanted the Psalms in church do so with such a slight degree of cantillation—that is, recitation with musical tones—that it was more like speaking than singing. He writes:

> Yet again, when I remember the tears I shed at the Psalmody of Thy Church, in the beginning of my recovered faith; and how at this time I am moved, not with the singing, but with the things sung, when they are sung with a clear voice and modulation most suitable, I acknowledge the great use of this institution. Thus I fluctuate between peril of pleasure and approved wholesomeness; inclined the rather (though not as pronouncing an irrevocable opinion) to approve of the usage of singing in the church; that so by the delight of the ears the weaker minds might rise to the feeling of devotion. Yet when it befalls me to be more moved with the voice than with the words sung, I confess to have sinned penally, and then had rather not hear music. See now my state; weep with me, and weep for me, ye, whoso regulate your feelings within, as that good action ensues. For you who do not act, these things touch you not. But Thou, O Lord my God, hearken; behold and see, and have mercy and heal me, Thou, in whose presence I have become a problem to myself; and that is my infirmity.[10]

He writes (and confesses) as one who has a profound right-brain appreciation of music. The church's music sends him into raptures. But he does not seem to understand, as many do not today, that there might be a valid nonverbal message coming from God through the music, quite apart from the words. Is it OK habitually to ignore the words sung in corporate worship? Of course not. One would then be publicly affirming and confessing all sorts of things unintentionally to God and others.

But is it always wrong to be so moved by the music that the words become secondary? Again, no. Since we have been created with both hemispheres of the brain, God must place great value on the data each side can uniquely send and apprehend. Just as there are times when only words will do, there are also times when no

words can express what must be expressed. I often find myself wishing that Augustine had understood that better. His guilty feelings as expressed above do not seem in my view to be necessarily warranted. Yet it must be said, considering the lustfulness of his earlier life, perhaps his problems with music in worship were more sinful than I realize. God alone will be his judge and mine.

At any rate, Augustine seems fully to understand that words cannot say everything that needs to be said:

> Sing *in jubilation*: singing well to God means, in fact just this: singing in jubilation. What does singing in jubilation signify? It is to realize that words cannot communicate the song of the heart. Just so singers in the harvest, or the vineyard, or at some other arduous toil express their rapture to begin with in songs set to words; then, as if bursting with a joy so full that they cannot give vent to it in set syllables, they drop actual words and break into the free melody of pure jubilation. The *jubilus* is a melody which conveys that the heart is in travail over something it cannot bring forth in words. And to whom does that jubilation rightly ascend, if not to God the ineffable? Truly is He ineffable whom you cannot tell forth in speech; and if you cannot tell him forth in speech, yet ought not to remain silent, what else can you do but jubilate? In this way the heart rejoices without words and the boundless expanse of rapture is not circumscribed by syllables. *Sing well to him in jubilation.*[11]

Augustine obviously knew little about the structure of the human brain, but he was perceptive about the varied ways his brain was working. And he expresses quite clearly the cultural and religious conflicts that often arise from such dichotomies. Indeed, he lived his life caught between these tensions.

Icons: East versus West

My teaching colleague Donald Fairbairn, professor of historical theology at Erskine Seminary, has recently published a book the burden of which is to describe Eastern Orthodoxy in ways that will make sense to those of us in the West. He takes considerable pains

to explain how differently the West and the East look at life. In certain ways, the difference can be understood in terms of varying styles of thinking involving different parts of the brain. He writes:

> [O]ne of the prominent differences between the way Easterners and Westerners view the world is that Westerners are (or at least were) more text-oriented, whereas Easterners are more image-oriented. . . . The Orthodox believe tradition is expressed through visual as well as textual means. . . .
>
> American Christians obey the Augustinian injunction "Take up and read!" Their Russian counterparts are apt to concentrate upon the insight that follows the imperative "Look up and see!"[12]

The tension between the left-brained world of words as opposed to the right-brained world of images is a central theme throughout his book. One of the most controversial issues separating Eastern Christianity from Western has been the use of icons— paintings of saints and of the persons of the Holy Trinity that are used by the Eastern church for purposes of veneration and meditation. In the eighth and ninth centuries, the Christian church was embroiled in a huge debate over the use of icons. For some, the veneration of, and even the very existence of, icons was a breaking of the second of the Ten Commandments, "Thou shalt not make unto thee any graven images . . . bow down, or worship them." However, others saw a clear difference between worship, which was reserved for the Trinity alone, and veneration, which was more of an honoring than an act of worship. Further, they argued, since Jesus is God revealed in visible form, the door is now open to make fuller use of visual representations of him.

Though the church eventually decided in A.D. 843 not to disallow the use of icons, they remain to this day one of the primary distinguishing features of Eastern and Western Christianity. Fairbairn takes pains to show that the two mind-sets about how reality is perceived have created not only radically different approaches to theology but also a stubbornly persistent inability for one side to even hear what the other side is really saying. As a result, many perceived differences between East and West are based not so much on substantial disagreements, but on each side's speaking "over the heads" of the other.

Fairbairn continues:

> In addition to these distinctives, one other difference between
> Eastern and Western perspectives that is closely related to the role
> of saints and icons is what would be called the emphasis on "de-
> light" versus the stress on "utility." Westerners, whose thought is
> governed by practical, utilitarian concerns, are likely to ask whether
> a certain practice is necessary for Christian life; if the practice is
> not necessary, Westerners will perhaps reject it. The Eastern view
> of the world, in contrast, seeks to celebrate reality rather than to
> use it. Orthodox theologians argue that the sheer variety in our
> world indicates that God's approach to reality is one of delight,
> not merely usefulness. (Schmemann is said to have asked fre-
> quently, "Why the hippopotamus?") In light of this emphasis, the
> Orthodox would argue that while we do need each other and the
> saints as we progress toward the kingdom, the importance of saints
> and icons is not simply found in the question of how we use them.
> They are also a celebration of the world and of the life God has
> given the church, a reflection of the delight that leads God to give
> himself to his church abundantly.[13]

How interesting to note that whole cultures, even macro-cul-
tures, develop tendencies that favor or reject the full engagement of
certain parts of the brain.

The Abbey Church of St. Denis

Our next stop takes us just north of Paris to the ancient Abbey of
St. Denis, established in A.D. 475. The combined influence of the
monarchy and the abbey's powerful leader, Abbot Suger, led in 1135
to the reconstruction and refurbishment of the Abbey church. What
resulted was a grand edifice considered by many to be the first
place of worship built in full Gothic style.

Abbot Suger is normally not credited with possessing a very
acute theological mind, but he was a great lover of all that was
grand, eloquent, and beautiful.[14] Now, this combination of characteristics can be guaranteed to raise red flags for a great many in

ecclesiastical authority who would want the balance to tilt in the opposite direction. Suger is often dismissed as a pompous show-off, more interested in vainglory than in the true mission of the church. People of this persuasion would be all the more convinced of Suger's vanity were they to read the inscription chiseled at his direction above the front door of the church: "For the splendor of the church that has fostered and exalted him, Suger has labored for the splendor of the church. Giving thee a share of what is thine, O Martyr Denis, he prays to thee to pray that he may obtain a share of Paradise."[15]

Suger was a child of his age. This conclusion is obvious in the Medieval works-centered theology implicit in his engraving. He also shares the common medieval theological perspective that beautiful things have a sacramental potential to manifest the grace of God. But as we have seen, a balanced appreciation for the right brain's perspective (whether or not one shares that perspective) counsels against too hasty a negative judgment on the abbot. We get a fuller sense of his motivations as we continue reading his portal inscription:

> Whoever thou art, if thou seekest to extol the glory of these doors, marvel not at the gold and the expense but at the craftsmanship of the work. Bright is the noble work; but, being nobly bright, the work should brighten the minds, so that they may travel, through the true lights, to the True Light where Christ is the true door. . . . The dull mind rises to truth through that which is material and, seeing the light, is resurrected from its former submersion.[16]

One of the glories of the Gothic style is that advanced construction techniques allowed for much larger windows, and thus, much more light. Nothing in St. Denis was designed without a theological purpose. From the relative darkness of the narthex (entry vestibule), the entering worshipers would burst forth into the light of the nave, resplendent in the multicolors of the stained-glass windows. The worshipers would never have seen such a thing before, and the effect must have been stunning. Suger was thrilled to see the reaction of his congregation as the faithful internalized the obvious connection with the glory of heaven and of Christ, the Light

of the World. And, as we can surmise from Suger's inscription—from his perspective as an educated Medieval man, as well as a man whose thinking had some strong right-brained components—material things, nonverbal things (that is, things perceived through the senses) had a great power to elevate "dull minds" to truth.

John Newton versus George Frideric Handel

As Suger's cathedral embodied the Gothic ideal, our next example embodies the Baroque. George Frideric Handel's oratorio *Messiah* caused no small stir in the cultural and religious life of London in 1741 and thereafter. At the heart of the hubbub was whether a musical work with a sacred text—and a text about Jesus Christ, at that—might properly be performed as a piece of concert music in a theater where operas were usually performed. For secularists, the controversy was simply about matters of taste or propriety. For the Christian community, however, deeper issues were at stake. Was this concert not an affront to God? Was it not a sin to perform sacred music in a concert hall? This was, it must be remembered, an England still less than 100 years distant from Cromwell's Puritan Commonwealth. Many religious people, whether Puritan or Anglican, refrained from any theatergoing whatever, for conscience's sake. Other people of faith, such as Handel himself and his librettist, Charles Jennens, saw no conflict or affront here. And these differences of opinion, once again, have to do with the relative importance of words and music.

One famous person who had more than a few reservations was John Newton, best known for his hymn text "Amazing Grace." Newton freely admitted that Handel was a great man and *Messiah* a stunning achievement. But it seemed to him that, as with Augustine's concern, the music diverted attention from the meaning of the text. Further, the typical audience that would come to hear the concert would probably have come for the wrong reasons—to enjoy the music rather than to consider the text. Such objections would be voiced in the case of any religious text performed in concert. But the issue was magnified many times over because the text in this instance was none other than an account of

the person and work of the Son of God. Finally, Newton objected that the theater was no place to perform such a work. "True Christians," he wrote, "without the assistance of either vocal or instrumental music, may find greater pleasure in a humble contemplation on the *words* of *Messiah*, than they can derive from the utmost efforts of musical genius. . . . Those who have received pleasure from the music of *Messiah*, have neither found, nor expected, nor desired to find, any comfort from the words."[17]

Newton, an active preacher and pastor, writes with that sense of frustration many pastors confess as they pour their hearts and very lives into sermons that so often seem to have little effect. He may even be feeling a bit of jealousy. In one of his sermons, he complains:

> *Messiah* is but an ornament of the words, which have a very weighty sense [that] no music can explain, and when rightly understood, will have such an effect as no music can produce. [The words], divested of the music, when delivered from the pulpit, are heard by many admirers of the oratorio with indifference, too often with contempt.[18]

As much as we might relate to Newton's concerns, I see some need for refutation here, not so much because he is wrong as because he seems unable to see the whole picture. Yes, any musical setting of a text might deflect attention from the text to the musical setting. However, the music might as easily provide fresh insights into the text, providing at times an exposition that words alone could not.

Yes, it is fair to assume that many in those theater audiences came for the music and not to adore the risen Christ. Their disregard of this presentation of the gospel was one more sinful rejection on their part. But to make a blanket claim that the entire audience came for the wrong reasons goes far beyond what even as saintly a man as John Newton could know. He is almost certainly wrong about that, if he meant it literally. Further, it might be considered an evangelistic coup to get so many secular souls to sit through a three-hour presentation of the Christian gospel, especially since every word sung comes straight from the Holy Scriptures. In a similar

way, C. S. Lewis wrote children's stories and science-fiction novels that give every appearance of being secular, yet are actually intended surreptitiously to inculcate the reader with the basic truths of the Christian faith. Some believe that Lewis's Christian friend, J. R. R. Tolkien, in his own much more subtle, nonallegorical way, fills his Lord of the Rings trilogy with mega-themes that reinforce major biblical themes.

Newton, like so many, seems to sell short the God-given specialties of the right brain. It seems not to cross his mind that times and situations occur in which God might be inclined to confront us through the right rather than the left hemisphere. Of course, he would not know of such biological distinctions, but his dismissal of right-brain-formatted information is typical of those who cannot conceive how nonverbal communication can be of equal value to verbal.

Unfortunately, when this sort of dismissal comes from one in authority, those whose brains God "wired" differently from the leader's confront an ongoing struggle to learn and grow, using less acute portions of their brains. Of course, the good news is that if these people persevere under these constraints, they often end up the stronger, since this constant exercise of these less-acute brain centers strengthens them. Thus, in a culture where word- and logic-oriented educational systems clearly dominate, visually oriented people may develop better balance and integration of multiple brain centers than those who are already word-oriented.

C. S. Lewis and Whole-Brainedness

As we have just mentioned C. S. Lewis above, let us now consider his work in more detail. "'Would not conversation be much more rational than dancing?' said Jane Austen's Miss Bingley. 'Much more rational,' replied Mr. Bingley, 'but much less like a ball.'" Lewis uses this quotation in his famous essay "Myth Became Fact,"[19] to help us come to terms with his understanding of the dynamic relationship between rationality and imagination.

It would be hard to find an individual in the twentieth century who gave greater evidence of holistic balance between the cerebral

hemispheres than C. S. Lewis. A study of his life reveals how many of life's experiences strengthen our use of various thought centers of the brain.

As a child Lewis spent hours creating an imaginary kingdom that he called Animal Land. He and his brother, Warren, wrote extensive chapters developing the history of the place, its geography, and its people. The people, of course, were animals—talking animals that wore clothes like humans. The pages of Animal Land were replete with painted drawings of the inhabitants and maps of their kingdom. In Lewis's own words, "I can remember no time when we were not incessantly drawing."[20] He was also incessantly reading. "Nothing was forbidden," he writes of the mountains of books to be found throughout his childhood home. "In the seemingly endless rainy afternoons I took volume after volume from the shelves."[21] As Lewis grew, he gained an interest in poetry, and well into adulthood his chief desire for his career was to be a poet. It is not hard to see, therefore, how such a fellow might grow up to write engaging novels about a magical kingdom called Narnia, where animals can talk and where the great hero is a lion named Aslan. Lewis's imagination was alive and well.

But so was his prowess in reason and logic. And what was naturally a part of his mental profile was sharpened through rigorous training. In his autobiography, *Surprised by Joy*, Lewis describes his first attempt at conversation with his relentlessly left-brained new tutor, Mr. Kirkpatrick, The Great Knock:

> "You are now," said Kirk, "proceeding along the principal artery between Great and Little Bookham." I proceeded to "make conversation" in the deplorable manner which I had acquired at those evening parties. . . . I said I was surprised at the "scenery" of Surrey; it was much "wilder" than I had expected.
>
> "Stop!" shouted Kirk with a suddenness that made me jump. "What do you mean by wildness and what grounds had you for not expecting it?"
>
> I replied I don't know what, still "making conversation." As answer after answer was torn to shreds it at last dawned upon me that he really wanted to know. He was not making conversation, nor joking, nor snubbing me; he wanted to know. I was stung

into attempting a real answer. A few passes sufficed to show that I had no clear and distinct idea corresponding to the word "wildness," and that, in so far as I had any idea at all, "wildness" was a singularly inept word. "Do you not see, then," concluded the Great Knock, "that your remark was meaningless?" I prepared to sulk a little, assuming that the subject would now be dropped. Never was I more mistaken in my life. Having analyzed my terms, Kirk was proceeding to deal with my proposition as a whole. On what had I based (but he pronounced it *baized*) my expectations about the Flora and Geology of Surrey. Was it maps, or photographs, or books? I could produce none. It had, heaven help me, never occurred to me that what I called my thoughts needed to be "baized" on anything. Kirk once more drew a conclusion—without the slightest sign of emotion, but equally without the slightest concession to what I thought good manners: "Do you now see then, that you had no right to have any opinion whatever on the subject?"

By this time our acquaintance had lasted about three and a half minutes; but the tone set by this first conversation was preserved without a single break during all the years I spent at Bookham. . . .

If ever a man came near to being a purely logical entity, that man was Kirk. Born a little later, he would have been a Logical Positivist. The idea that human beings should exercise their vocal organs for any purpose except that of communicating or discovering truth was to him preposterous. The most casual remark was taken as a summons to disputation. . . .

Some boys would not have liked it; to me it was red beef and strong beer. . . . The only two kinds of talk I wanted were the almost purely imaginative and the almost purely rational. . . . Kirk excited and satisfied one side of me.[22]

It seems to me that one of the reasons the writings of C. S. Lewis have had such a profound effect on so many varied sorts of people is that he was a master at appealing to multiple portions of the brain. Some books, like *Mere Christianity*, appeal more to the logical; others, like his Space Trilogy, appeal more to the imaginative. But virtually every book he wrote has a way of constantly

engaging both the rational and the imaginative, the concrete and the metaphoric. This dual emphasis in his writing did not happen by accident. Although he did not speak of left and right brains, he gave ample proof of not only understanding the distinction but of purposefully utilizing both. He writes:

> It must not be supposed that I am in any sense putting forward the imagination as the organ of truth. We are not talking of truth, but of meaning: meaning which is the antecedent condition both of truth and falsehood, whose antithesis is not error but nonsense. . . . For me, reason is the natural organ of truth; but imagination is the organ of meaning. Imagination, producing new metaphors or revivifying old, is not the cause of truth, but its condition.[23]

For Lewis, reason has to do with theoretical propositions, while the meanings assigned to these propositions, these "truths," are applied by the imagination. Each needs the other. He would say that poor meanings make for poor thoughts.

He argued further that the organization of truths into propositions requires the use of all manner of subjective metaphors that come from the imagination. One can get a fuller explanation of this concept in his book *Miracles*, where he proposes that to speak of anything that goes beyond what our five human senses can perceive requires the use of metaphoric language. He observes that we talk of such things as institutions or mental complexes "as if they could be seen or touched or heard." We speak of our desires as if they could be "shoved back" or of institutions developing as if they were trees or unfolding flowers, or of energy being released "as if it were an animal let out of a cage." But in fact, we do not literally shove back our feelings; it is merely a helpful picture of something that is *like* what we do with our feelings. We find ourselves over and over in the world of simile and metaphor.[24]

Lewis writes of this important role for the imagination in his autobiographical allegory, *The Pilgrim's Regress*. Toward the end of the book, John the Pilgrim (Lewis, actually) hears a Voice at his baptism: "The words of Wisdom are also myth and metaphor. . . . But this is my inventing, this is the veil under which I have chosen

to appear even from the first until now. For this end I made your senses and for this end your imagination, that you might see my Face and live."[25]

Thus Lewis shows the necessary interplay between imagination and rationality. Most mental enterprises would be virtually blocked without this vital interplay. In the final stop in our world tour, we find another who placed great value on the imaginative as well as rational. His identity may surprise you.

Albert Einstein's Education

Had we encountered Albert Einstein as a high-school student, we would probably not have marked him for fame and greatness. Historians differ in their appraisal of his early education, but it seems clear that he was frustrated by the strict, generally verbal rote approach of the late-nineteenth-century German academic system. He did not learn to speak until much later than most children and seems to have had trouble with verbalization in general. He later explained:

> The words or the language, as they are written or spoken, do not seem to play any role in my mechanism of thought. The psychical entities which seem to serve as elements in thought are certain signs and more or less clear images which can be "voluntarily" produced and combined. . . . The above mentioned elements are, in my case, of visual and some of muscular type. Conventional words or other signs have to be sought for laboriously only in a secondary stage, when the mentioned associative play is sufficiently established and can be reproduced at will. [26]

Einstein's academic difficulties were not the result of his being a late bloomer. He was one of many young people caught in an educational system that focused rather exclusively on limited learning techniques—reading, lecture, reason, and analysis. He said, later in life, "The only thing that interferes with my learning is my education." He explained why this was so: "The intuitive mind is a sacred gift and the rational mind is a faithful servant. We have

created a society that honors the servant and has forgotten the gift. The only real valuable thing is intuition. The gift of fantasy has meant more to me than my talent or absorbing positive knowledge." Elsewhere he summarizes this philosophy: "After a certain high level of technical skill is achieved, science and art tend to coalesce in aesthetics, plasticity, and form. The greatest scientists are always artists as well."[27] In fact, on occasion Einstein could be seen jumping up in the middle of a piece he was playing on the violin to scribble down some idea or equation that popped into his head while making music.

While I suspect that the situation is generally much better today in Western educational systems, my observation, based on a lifetime of association with public and private education, is that there is still a significant bias in favor of left-brained teaching and learning techniques. One indication of this predisposition comes from recent studies done on the creativity of young children. On tests of creativity, young children usually score quite high. But creativity declines by 40 percent between the ages of five and seven.[28] These are, of course, the ages when children have their first experiences with school. Many factors might account for this statistic, but most experts agree that the effects of formal education are impossible to overlook. Among the factors that experts agree stifle creativity are working under surveillance, having only limited choices, working for rewards not closely related to the tasks at hand, fearing failure, knowing that one will be evaluated, feeling a need to compete, and working under pressure.

A Call For Balance

These examples show how tensions between right-brain and left-brain styles of thinking have been central to the human experience throughout history. They also give fuller insight into the natures of each cerebral hemisphere. Although these examples might seem to suggest that I favor the right brain, my hope is to correct the general Western cultural bias in favor of the left brain. We live in a culture in which formal education relies overwhelmingly on lectures, verbal and mathematical skills, retention of facts, objective

testing, and the scientific empirical method. While in recent years we have seen an increasing interest in more right-brained approaches to learning and knowing, the Western world still seems to place greater value on left-brained mental pursuits.

My intention is to argue for equal respect for the essential contributions made by both sides of our brain and for the intentions of our Creator, who had good reasons for designing it in that way. Such respect would manifest itself in a creative, reverent, and vital commitment to worship that does more than demonstrate our loyalties to tradition or denomination on one hand, or our desire for contemporary relevance on the other. I believe that modern brain research gives us one more valid tool to use as we continue our rather tempestuous search for the mind of God regarding Christian worship.

Thus far, we have based our exploration of this issue primarily on the findings of brain research experts. But what of the sources Christians rightly depend upon for guidance about matters of faith, such as worship? What of the Holy Scriptures and the insights of great theologians? Having established a basic understanding of the issues at hand, it is now our task to integrate them with the foundational truths of biblical Christianity.

Questions for Thought and Discussion

1. What people from the Bible, history, or your life experience have influenced your *knowing* and *experiencing* God? What has each contributed to your spiritual formation?

2. From your educational experience, list various literary works that have shaped your thinking. List literary works that have puzzled or confused you.

3. Explore your patterns of learning. As you consider art, music, even dance classes in juxtaposition to history, mathematics, science, and philosophy, begin to think through patterns of learning in each of these disciplines. Identify those beneficial to your development and those that have been bothersome or tedious.

4. Revisit C.S. Lewis's quote: "For me, reason is the natural organ of truth; but imagination is the organ of meaning."

Define *reason* and *imagination* in your own words. What part does each play in your experience of corporate worship? How is each beneficial in your spiritual formation?

5. Discuss the commandment "Thou shalt not make unto thee any graven image" and your views regarding the use of non-verbal symbols in worship.

Chapter Three

The Biblical Call for Hemispheric Balance

These commandments that I give you today are to be upon your hearts. Impress them on your children. Talk about them when you sit at home and when you walk along the road, when you lie down and when you get up.

—*Deuteronomy 6:6, 7*

See, I have chosen Bezalel son of Uri . . . and I have filled him with the Spirit of God, with skill, ability and knowledge in all kinds of crafts.

—*Exodus 31:2, 3*

We do not know what we ought to pray for, but the Spirit himself intercedes for us with groans that words cannot express.

—*Romans 8:26*

One of the first things you learn when undertaking a serious study of the Bible is that it is composed of various kinds of literature. The Bible includes law codes, theological treatises, prophetic visions and utterances, apocalyptic, and various types of poetry.

Different literary forms call upon different parts of the brain. For example, law codes and theological treatises are rationalistic, sequential, logical, and analytical. Such thought patterns tend to engage more left-brain centers. Poetry and apocalyptic tend to engage more right-brain centers. They use metaphor, word pictures, symbolism, and aesthetics. Historical narrative and prophetic visions often require a rich palette of both left- and right-brain thought patterns. The creation account in Genesis, for example, is considered

by some to be historical narrative, yet it is written in a poetic style. According to Bruce Waltke, Old Testament professor at Reformed Seminary in Orlando:

> The story is based on events in time and space, a real Adam and Eve. But it is not merely a historical account. The style is artistic and figurative rather than scientific and literalistic. The scenes of creation are painted as an artist might envision them: God, as a potter, forming the man; as a gardener, designing a garden of beauty and abundance; and as a temple builder, raising the woman from the rib of the man.
>
> The suprahistorical dimension is also essential for the theology of this account. On this register, Adam and Eve represent every man and woman (Gen. 3:16–19; cf. 2:24; Matt. 19:4–6; Rom. 5:12). They represent our own rebellion, fallenness, and need for God's graceful redemption. This is as important as the historical dimension. Therefore, both the historical and the suprahistorical should be held in proper tension.[1]

The stories of Moses, Joseph, and David are all considered to be historical narrative, and as such they rely primarily on left-brained sequential patterns of verbalization—first one event happens, then another, and another. Yet they are filled with visual imagery, and their ability to fire the imagination is one reason they make great children's stories. Prophecy is filled with logical accounts of why Israel has yet again failed. But the prophets were known to deliver their inspired poetic utterances in an ecstatic state aroused in part through music making. Ancient Hebrew poetry was never merely spoken, but sung. And Hebrew prophecy is generally written as poetry. Further, prophets are well known for their imaginative symbols—plumb lines, valleys filled with dry bones, all manner of strange beasts, and wheels within wheels.

The Biblical Use of "Mind, Soul, and Heart"

The title of this book echoes the famous response of Jesus to the question "What is the greatest commandment?" He answers by quoting a portion of the central affirmation of Judaism, the *Shema*,

as recorded in Deuteronomy 6:5: "Love the Lord your God with all your heart and with all your soul and with all your strength." Matthew 22:37 records a slightly different catalogue: "Love the Lord your God with all your heart and with all your soul and with all your mind." Mark 12:30 and Luke 10:27 list all four items— heart, soul, mind, and strength.

If one finds this inconsistency somewhat perplexing, it is even more puzzling to try to decipher exactly what is meant by *heart, soul,* and *mind.* The Hebrew word used for *heart* in Deuteronomy 6:5 is *leb.* It is considered the innermost organ, the center of a person. It is used in the Old Testament to refer to a wide variety of things in addition to the heart, including the will, feelings, even the intellect. But will, feelings, and intellect clearly relate to the mind as well, and in fact the Moffatt translation of the Bible uses the word *mind* for the Hebrew *leb* in this verse.

The Hebrew word generally translated as *mind* is *nephesh,* which, like *leb,* has multiple meanings, including the soul; the inner being; and the seat of the appetites, emotions, or passions.[2] It seems there is no distinct difference between the two Hebrew words themselves, and English translations of the Old Testament are filled with instances in which each of these Hebrew words, *nephesh* and *leb,* is translated both ways—"mind" and "heart." It is tempting to assume that these two words are basically synonyms, and in fact some scholars question whether a clear distinction existed even for the Old Testament writers themselves.[3] But there are Old Testament verses that do mention heart (*leb*) and mind (*nephesh*) as two separate things, just as the New Testament references to the *Shema* do. For example, 1 Samuel 2:35 states, "I will raise up for myself a faithful priest, who will do according to what is in my heart and mind." One would need to enter an ancient Hebrew mind-set to truly grasp all these subtleties.

We see from these word studies that though we cannot assign to biblical words such as *heart, soul,* and *mind* strictly right- or left-brain connotations, they still help establish the thesis of this book. Each of these words has wide ranges of meaning that include attributes of *both* hemispheres of the brain. And this is precisely the point. As we shall see in this chapter and the next, the Bible is the friend of all parts of the brain. Thus, the command to love God "with all thy mind" means exactly that—*all* of the mind—right

and left halves; front, middle, and back of the cerebral cortex; as well as the limbic brain and the archipallium or brain stem.

With the richness of this biblical language as our basis, let us now explore larger biblical themes that further exemplify the point.

The Imago Dei

Imago Dei, Latin for *the image of God,* refers to the passage in Genesis 1:27 where we read that "God created man in his own image." As we explore the implications of this verse, we will see that God uses a poetic format to describe the *imago,* thus engaging our minds holistically. We will also consider how human creativity in all its rich manifestations is a major component of the *imago.*

There is no getting around the simple truth that the God who conceived and created our brains takes great care to reveal himself in his Word in ways that would affect many aspects of the person, and consequently, different locations in the brain. That he also does so in the world at large through general revelation should be abundantly clear as well at this point.

Consider the implications of Genesis 1:27:

So God created man in his own image,
in the image of God he created him;
male and female he created them.

The first thing to notice is that this is not just simple prose. In fact it is an excellent example of Hebrew poetry. The Hebrew poetry of this time did not rhyme sounds but ideas, through a stylistic technique known as parallelism. In parallelism a simple statement is made in the first phrase, and the second phrase makes a corresponding response. While parallelism can be achieved in a number of ways, three patterns are used most frequently.

Synonymous parallelism simply restates the idea expressed in the first phrase. Psalm 103:1 (KJV) gives us a classic example of this type of parallelism:

> Bless the Lord, O my soul
> And all that is within me, bless his holy Name.

Notice that the second phrase repeats the first, but in reverse order. "Bless the Lord" parallels "bless his holy Name," and "O my soul" parallels "all that is within me."

In a second form, *antithetical parallelism*, the second phrase says basically the same thing as the first, but does so by means of contrasting opposites. The book of Proverbs is filled with examples of this category, such as Proverbs 10:16:

> The wages of the righteous bring them life,
> But the income of the wicked brings them punishment.

The third type is *synthetic parallelism*. Here the second phrase echoes the idea expressed in the first, but says it in a more concise way, narrowing the scope of meaning. Consider Psalm 90:8:

> You have set our iniquities before you,
> Our secret sins in the light of your presence.

Notice how the first phrase speaks of iniquities in general, while the second phrase narrows the scope to a particular category of iniquity—our secret sins.

Returning to our passage in Genesis 1, we are now prepared to analyze its poetic structure.

> So God created man in his own image,
> in the image of God he created him;
> male and female he created them.

We notice that it is a double parallelism—three phrases. Phrase 2 is an almost exact repetition of phrase 1, though the order is inverted, as in Psalm 103 above. This is a classic example of virtually pristine synonymous parallelism. The third phrase refines the meaning of "man" by revealing that "man" was created as male and female. This might be considered an example of synthetic parallelism.

Others might argue that the third phrase is really a second use of synonymous parallelism.

How intriguing that this verse introducing the idea of the *Imago Dei*, a verse of stupendous theological importance, is presented to us by divine inspiration in the form of poetry! For most biblical scholars, poetry is rarely the vehicle for theological discussion. It is felt to be too imprecise a mode of expression for expounding great truths.

Yet the entire three-chapter epic of creation and fall, as mentioned above, has strong poetic overtones. We note the lyricism of the oft-repeated phrases:

"And God said . . . ,"
"And there was evening and there was morning . . . ,"
". . . and God saw that it was good."

This litany continues to resonate in our ears and minds, building up to the ringing Grand Finale, "...and it was *very* good" (emphasis added).

Further, we have a parallel structure encompassing the entire first chapter. The first day of creation (light) correlates with the fourth day (lights in the sky); the second day (waters and sky) correlates with the fifth (water life and birds); the third day (dry ground) correlates with the fourth (land animals). The grand culmination is, of course, the creation of humankind, which stands alone without a corollary. Commentators see various ways to subdivide and interpret this and other parallelisms in Genesis 1–3, but the observations above are hard to refute and provide sufficient examples of poetic elements in Genesis.

Waltke draws our attention to a chiastic[4] structure in chapters two and three:

A—Creation of man: his happy relationship with the earth and his home in the garden, where he has freely growing food and access to the tree of life (2:4-17)
B—Creation of woman: her happy relationship with man (2:18-25)
C—Conversation of serpent with woman: his tempting of her (3:1-5)

X—The sin and God's uncovering of it (3:6-13)
C'—Punishment of serpent: its spoiled relationship with woman (3:14-15)
B'—Punishment of woman: her spoiled relationship with man (3:16)
A'—Punishment of man: his spoiled relationship with the earth and expulsion from his home in the garden; he now has to toil to secure food and will no longer have access to the tree of life (3:17-24).

This analysis exposes the crucial moment as Adam and Eve's choice to eat the forbidden fruit. The chiasm may justify combining acts 1 and 2 into one act: "the expulsion of man from the Garden." [5]

As can be readily seen in this first example, God takes special care to communicate his meaning in formats that engage multiple cognitive centers in the brain. While the general verbalization primarily engages the left side, the imagery and the various poetic elements engage the right.

Let us now explore the implications of the *imago* relative to human creativity. Just what it means to be created in the image of God has always been, of course, a topic of much debate. Many will say that it refers to the higher mental powers that humanity alone enjoys. Some might focus on human powers of reason or logic; others may suggest our ability to be aware of ourselves, our moral sensibilities, our sinless state before the fall of Adam and Eve, our spiritual natures, the immortality of our souls, or our dominion over the rest of creation.[6] I see no reason why it cannot include all the items listed above.

I must say that I have long wondered why creativity is not listed among the possible elements of the *Imago Dei*. I believe that creativity is a major manifestation of that Image in human beings. We believe and confess that God is the Creator of all things, visible and invisible. When we say that God is the Creator, we mean that God created all that *is*, and created it out of nothing. This is the meaning of the Hebrew word *bara*. While humans obviously do not create things out of nothingness, we have been endowed by God with various gifts of creativity. It is a characteristic that, to a considerable

though limited extent, we share with our Creator and with no other creature. Creativity is a significant part of what it means to have been created in the image of God.

One glorious characteristic about the things God creates is that they have aesthetic qualities. In short, they are beautiful. God does not create things that are simply functional. They do work beautifully (when not spoiled by humanity), but beyond that, they are so often a delight to the eye, ear, nose, touch, and taste. The vast world of nature is the obvious example. As modern science unlocks the mysteries of interstellar space and the equally vast atomic and sub-atomic worlds, we are regularly introduced to new examples of surpassing sensual and even mathematical beauty.

One of the most beautiful things I can imagine is our earth as seen from space. I have often seen the incredible IMAX movies shown on massive multi-storied screens at such places as the Kennedy Space Center and the Smithsonian Institution. And these secondhand glimpses are still enough to bring tears to my eyes. For whom did God make this beauty? For all the generations of humankind until our own, this sight was not possible. No one had ever seen it. So why did God "go to all the trouble" to make earth so breathtakingly beautiful? This is simply who God is. It is the nature of God to go beyond mere functionality in creation. God cannot but make things beautiful as well. And what is not beautiful is at least interesting and often funny. Have you been to the zoo lately?

Humans share this characteristic with God. While we do not *bara* (create) anything, we are inveterate "makers." We are constantly building, cooking, designing, knitting, grafting, cloning, sewing, composing, painting, and in general making something new. And like our creator, we are not satisfied to merely make our creations function well, though that is also important to us; we carve designs in what we make, we smear colored pigment over the designs, we round off the corners, add a sprig of parsley, stain and varnish, add frills, tassels, moldings, metaphors, chrome, spices, adverbs and adjectives, sequins, and froufrous. We do this to our chairs, clothing, football helmets, guns, appliances, and cars. We can't help ourselves. This is who we are. This is how God made us.

In Genesis 1 we learn that God made it all. We learn that God made it "very good." We learn that God designed and made our brains and that he intends to communicate with us through many cognitive avenues. We learn that we, male and female, are created in God's image and that means in part that we, too, need to communicate from and to all parts of both hemispheres of our God-given, God-designed brains.

God's Instructions about the Tabernacle

I know of no more poignant example of God's concern for aesthetics and creativity than the biblical account of the building of the Tabernacle. It is an amazing thing to consider the amount of space taken up in Holy Writ with details about the construction of this Tabernacle, and later, Solomon's Temple. No fewer than 13 chapters, Exodus 25-31 and 35-40, concern themselves with nothing other than the details of the construction of the Tabernacle, its furnishings, and the priestly garments. Precious few topics in Scripture are covered in such detail. The first 10 chapters in Leviticus give commands about the sacrificial system and the ordination of priests; 1 Kings 5-8 offers the account of the building of Solomon's Temple—and a host of chapters scattered throughout the Pentateuch provide additional instruction on matters of worship.

Whatever else we make of these vast accounts, it must be agreed that they bear striking testimony to the importance God places on matters of divine worship. As we consider the explicit instructions given by the Lord for the building of the Tabernacle, we are confronted with some rather amazing statistics:

1. The project required just over one ton of gold, three and three-fourths tons of silver, and two and a half tons of bronze to overlay most of the wooden sections of the structure and the furnishings—all this for a portable tent and its furnishings!
2. God specifically calls for the following ornamentation for the tabernacle, its furnishings, and the priestly robes:

a. horns on the altar (ch. 27),

b. perfumed incense (ch. 30),

c. perfumed anointing oil (ch. 30),

d. colored linen of gold, blue, purple, and scarlet (throughout the passage),

e. pomegranates on the blue hem of the priest's ephod (ch. 28),

f. bells of gold between the pomegranates all around the hems of the priest's ephod (ch 28),

g. various artistic designs that seems to be left up to the artists. (ch. 31),

h. embroidery (ch. 31),

i. cherubim on curtains and veil (ch. 26), two cherubim on the Ark of the Covenant (ch. 25),

j. almond blossoms, branches, and flowers on the lamp stand (ch. 25),

k. two onyx stones with the names of the tribes placed in gold filigree for the priest's ephod (ch. 28),

l. 12 precious gemstones for the priest's breastpiece (ch. 28),

m. a plate of pure gold with "Holiness unto the Lord" engraved upon it for the priest's turban (ch. 28), and

n. no less than 11 times in this passage God repeats his command to use *skillful* workers.

3. This is the first account we have in Scripture of someone's being "filled with the Spirit" (Exod. 31:3) to do a certain task.

Can you imagine the typical American Protestant church constructing a building with such opulence? Of course, the Tabernacle was not designed to be in any way typical. Its closest American counterpart would have to be something like the Capitol in Washington, D.C. It was the epicenter of the budding nation of Israel, as Solomon's Temple most certainly was to be later on. But while the wealth required to build the Tabernacle is impressive, the real issue is about a different sort of opulence—not an opulence of material

wealth, but an aesthetic opulence. We meet here an aspect of the Divine Personality that has been, frankly, ignored or at least over-looked by much of Protestantism in general. Here is a God keenly interested in the sensual world. Here is a God who is a patron of the arts. Here is a God who commands over and over that the artists and workers must be skillful. It is seemingly of vital impor-tance to God that worshipers be able to apprehend God holisti-cally, with their entire selves—including all their senses.

They are to see the grandeur of the Tabernacle, its furnishings, priestly garments, and ceremonies; appreciate the beauty; and be instructed and reminded by the symbolism. Exodus 28:40 even states (at least in some translations) that the priests' garments were to be "for glory and for beauty."[7] The worshipers are to hear the glori-ous cacophony of the bells on the priestly garments, the sounds of animals led to sacrifice and being slaughtered, the sounds of shofar and festival trumpets, the Levitical choirs and instrumentalists min-istering during the sacrifices, the noise of the crowds. They could not help but smell all the animal odors—droppings, blood, roast-ing meat and internal organs; the acridity of whole burnt offerings. Perhaps they might catch a whiff of the incense used in the inner temple. The senses of touch and taste are included as the person offering the sacrifice must himself place his hand on the head of the animal and slit its throat (Lev. 1:4, 5). Fellowship offerings gave opportunities for the families to share a meal with the priest.

Here is a worship experience light years away from our mod-ern, relatively sterile, passive, word-dominant services of worship. In what ways do our typical twenty-first century worship encoun-ters similarly engage the whole person and draw us in? There is a fair amount of stimulation for our ears but not so much for our eyes, and precious little for our senses of taste, touch, and smell. Many traditions become immediately suspicious of worship that features much nonverbal stimulation. Students in my seminary worship classes are required to design their ideal worship space and explain why they have designed the room as they did. Many comment that they desire to keep visual artwork or symbolism to a minimum because they feel that it is a distraction to worship. Upon further examination, it becomes clear that what many of them mean

is that it might be a distraction from the sermon and other verbal aspects of the service.

As I understand these biblical accounts, God would have us see a much broader picture of what worship might be. Could it be that the same Spirit who infused these builders with skill not just to build but also to teach others their skills (Exod. 35:34) is being quenched by a well-intentioned refusal to consider the value God places on artistic expression? Worse still, the Spirit is sometimes more severely quenched by condemning nonverbal forms of worship as sinful. Has God changed? If our Creator exhibited such great concern about these things then, why not now? Exodus 28:43 states that the wearing of the priestly garments was to be a "lasting ordinance." With these considerations in mind, and the fact that the entire tabernacle and its accoutrements, even though portable, were designed to last, it seems safe to say that God's aesthetic concerns are also "lasting concerns."

What about the rest of Scripture? What other evidence might we find for God's desire to engage our entire minds?

Orpheus among the Prophets

In Greek mythology, Orpheus is the great musician whose singing sends all who hear into raptures, and who even has mystical power over inanimate objects. He is the very personification of music. A close look at biblical prophecy reveals that God's prophets as well had strong connections with poetry and music.

A surprisingly large portion of Old Testament prophecy is poetic in nature. Major portions of Isaiah, Jeremiah, and Ezekiel are written in the style of Hebrew poetry. Virtually all of Hosea, Joel, Amos, Obadiah, Micah, Nahum, Habakkuk, and Zephaniah are set as poetry. In these books we find a rather full compendium of Hebrew poetic styles—epithalamia (nuptial songs), lamentations, satirical poetry, and odes. The basic structure of Hebrew poetry—parallelism—permeates these books.

We will establish in the next chapter that the aesthetic and symbolic elements of poetry have strong connections with the right hemisphere of the brain, even though most verbal skills are cen-

tered in the left side. What is more, ancient Eastern cultures always *sang* poetry. It would never have entered the ancient Middle Eastern mind to *say* a poem. Thus, we see that biblical poetry is inherently musical as well. The very definition of the Hebrew word for *prophecy* is "to speak *(or sing)* by inspiration."[8]

Thus, as we imagine all those colorful accounts of prophets entering into ecstatic states, we should assume that those prophecies included a strong musical dimension. This is not to say that prophets *always* used music with their inspired utterances and writings; not all written prophecy is poetic in style. But most is. And in that culture, where there was poetry, there was music. Certainly, the account of David appointing the temple musicians in 1 Chronicles 25:1–3 makes this connection clear. And though it can be argued that the type of prophecy these temple musicians engaged in was of a different order than that of other prophets, Scripture still clearly labels it "prophecy."

We see other right-brained characteristics in biblical prophecy. God often chose to reveal his will to the prophets in visions and dreams. They were, in fact, called "seers." These visions were generally symbolic and needed interpretation to be understood. Then, these prophets were often known to use visual illustrations to deliver their messages. Jeremiah sees budding almond branches, boiling pots, and baskets of figs; God speaks to him through the work of a potter; he walks the streets of Jerusalem with yokes on his neck. The writings of the prophets are replete with such visions and visual illustrations.

Is there a direct linkage between these prophets and Christian worship? Yes and no. There is no biblical command that the prophets should do these things as part of any act of corporate worship. Yet the message is clear that God relies on much more than mere words to communicate with us. Should we do any less in our modern proclamation of God's Word?

Consider as well the way people read in the ancient world. Reading was done aloud, even if one was alone. Homer and Virgil—poets—were the bedrock of much of the ancient educational process. And because their poems were read aloud, the innate lyricism in their works was much more obvious. Reading was a matter not only of the eyes, as in modern Western culture, but of the tongue

and ears as well. The importance of hearing a passage read was
further intensified in that the ancients did not put spaces between
their written words. It was therefore much easier to get the sense
by sounding the words out rather than simply relying on the eye.

Because of this multisensual nature of reading, interpretation
of a text was a matter as much for the ear as for the eye. Subtleties
of interpretation could be made that would escape the notice of
those who relied only on sight. This practice may explain to some
degree why the biblical interpretations of certain church fathers
often strike us as forced. Their use of allusions and allegory comes
from a world where inner harmonies of a text were propounded as
much by the oratorical style of inflection, timing, and accent as by
mere written words on a page.[9] In short, *hearing* a passage read
well can engage many more parts of the brain than reading the
same passage silently to oneself.

The discussion above may seem a bit esoteric or contrived to
some. But the intention is to demonstrate the ways in which music
and poetry are deeply embedded in God's Word and in the history
of its interpretation. The God revealed in Scripture is not just a
wordsmith but an artist. To miss or to discard this point is to miss
out on much of what God has to say. But we have yet other dimensions of nonverbal divine revelation to explore.

Rainbows, Circumcision, Wine, and Bread

Isn't it interesting that God often provides a visual sign as accom-
paniment to a promise? Martin Luther, in explaining the Eucharist,
said of Jesus's words, "In all his promises, moreover, in addition to
the word, God has usually given a sign, for the greater assurance
and strengthening of our faith."[10] God promises never again to destroy the world with a flood. One would think the Almighty's word
on the deal would be enough. But God is gracious to overflowing.
Therefore, we are provided a rainbow, which for Noah, and everyone who follows, is forever associated with that promise. The rainbow not only symbolizes a promise not to flood the world again,
but also comes as a reminder of all God's promises in general. And,
by the way, it is ravishingly beautiful.

God establishes the Covenant with Abraham and with his descendants. He will be their God; they will be his people. The sign, circumcision, is to be inscribed on their very bodies (that is, of the men). The sign may not be so beautiful this time, but nonetheless it becomes the official sign of the Covenant. Israel's prophets, priests, and kings all are anointed with oil as a sign that God has chosen them and placed his Spirit upon them. According to God's instructions in Exodus 30:22, the anointing oil was to be the work of a perfumer. While this does not prove that the oil was given a scent, it seems pretty logical that this is why God assigned the job to a perfumer. I attended a healing service several years ago in which I was anointed with a scented oil. It was a profound experience not only at the time, but for days thereafter. The oil was absorbed into the skin of my forehead, and even my daily baths did not obliterate the olfactory reminder of God's promises. I can only imagine the effect of anointing as done in Old Testament times:

> How good and pleasant it is when brothers live together in
>   unity!
> It is like precious oil poured on the head,
> running down on the beard,
> running down on Aaron's beard,
> down upon the collar of his robes.
>
> Psalm 133:1, 2

Jesus institutes the sacraments of Holy Communion. He says at the Last Supper, "This is my blood of the covenant, which is poured out for many for the forgiveness of sins. I tell you, I will not drink of this fruit of the vine from now on until that day when I drink it anew with you in my Father's kingdom" (Matt. 26:28, 29).

Bread and wine: body and blood. Here is the ultimate in metaphor, in symbolism, in nonverbal communication. John Calvin writes of this Sacrament:

> It seems to me that a simple and proper definition would be to say
> that [a sacrament] is an outward sign by which the Lord seals on
> our consciences the promises of his good will toward us in order
> to sustain the weakness of our faith; and in turn attest our piety

toward him in the presence of the Lord and of his angels and before men.[11]

Here Calvin is echoing Augustine, who first laid out the simple definition of a sacrament as "a visible sign of an invisible grace." Similarly, the waters of baptism serve as sign and seal of God's promises of cleansing and rebirth to all who will believe.

In all these visible, sensual ways, God underscores words of promise to us. The signs are a part of the promise. In fact, the signs *are* the promise spoken by God himself to those nonverbal parts of the brain that specialize in that sort of communication.

Jesus and Parables

As we consider the writings of the New Testament, we notice a striking difference between the teaching style of Jesus and that of Paul, the chief writer of the Epistles. Mark reports in his Gospel, "With many similar parables Jesus spoke the word to them, as much as they could understand. *He did not say anything to them without using a parable.* But when he was alone with his own disciples, he explained everything" (Mark 4:33, 34, italics added). Clearly one of the main features of Jesus's teaching was his use of these simple stories to illustrate a lesson or truth. Parables are metaphoric, symbolic, and therefore right-brained. If we are seeking the left-brained systematic logic of a detailed theological argument, we need to turn to Paul. Again, we must be careful not to take this example too far. Jesus is certainly capable of using flawless logic, and Paul's writing is not without colorful illustrations. He makes use of numerous poems or hymns in his writing as well.

What warrants our careful attention, however, is Mark's surprisingly sweeping assertion that Jesus did not say *anything* to his disciples without the use of parables. The passage in Mark 4 is not completely clear as to whether this assertion refers to how Jesus taught the crowds in general or just the disciples. But either way, we are informed that this sort of storytelling was absolutely fundamental to Jesus's teaching style.

Parables engage the right side of the brain in at least two ways. First, they are rich in imagery. Our mind's eye is presented with intriguing vignettes of widows sweeping floors looking for coins, people burying pearls in fields, or prodigal sons slopping pigs. The pictures these vignettes produce in our minds are formulated in the right side of our brain.

Second, Jesus's parables always come with some sort of introduction. He might say, "The Kingdom of God is like a mustard seed," and then proceed with the parable. Or the parable might be introduced with a question someone asks: "Who is my neighbor?" The introduction contains clues as to how to interpret the story, and logic will not take the hearer very far in finding the meaning or the connecting links. It takes imagination to make the linkage between mustard seeds and the kingdom, and it often requires no small amount of mental energy to ferret out the meaning. Parables make us work, and the right side of the brain gets most of the workout. We are told that Jesus said nothing to his followers without using this sort of right-brain gymnastics.

A Whole Bible for a Whole Mind

What a magnificent spectrum of communicative devices is afforded us in the Bible! The One who inspired these Holy Scriptures is the same One who designed and created the human brain. We ought not be surprised that for every rationalistic discourse about grace, there is an imaginative parable elsewhere about grace. For every book like Romans, Galatians, and Ephesians, there is an Ecclesiastes, a Song of Solomon, or a Revelation.

The intent of this chapter has been to demonstrate the ways the faithful interpretation of Holy Scripture requires both right- and left-brain ways of thinking, and to show that such balance must exist if our perceptions and worship of God are to exhibit the abundant life God originally planned. Subsequent chapters demonstrate how much of modern worship seems to favor one side of the brain or the other. A worship tradition overfocused on right-brained modes of perception is no better, no healthier, no more biblical

than one overfocused on left-brained modes. It seems all too often that much of Christian worship has leaned too far in one direction or the other. It is much easier to find examples of imbalance than to find examples that engage the human brain holistically.

We turn our attention now to more purely theological matters. We have this biblical account. How shall we interpret this witness? How have some of the great thinkers of the Christian faith dealt with the biblical account as it relates to these issues? That is the subject of the next two chapters.

Questions for Thought and Discussion

1. Compare your personal definitions of "heart" and "soul" with the author's interpretation of the Hebrew words. Based on those definitions, attempt to identify whether your worship experiences are more right or left brained. To what extent is your worship a balanced combination of all aspects of the brain, including the cerebral cortex as well as the limbic brain and the archipallium or brain stem?

2. Spend extended time in the Proverbs and Psalms exploring the creative ways God has designed you "in his image." As you read, does the imagery speak to your soul? Do you begin to adjust the imagery into thought or word form, systematizing the information you are gleaning into theological categories? Or as you read, does your brain paint vivid pictures from the words of Scripture?

3. Consider your reading skills. Do you verbalize each word as you read? Do you find your lips moving as your eyes absorb words on the written page? Do you read every word or do you grasp the overall meaning of a paragraph as your eyes skip words and sentences?

4. Discuss your agreement or disagreement with the author's interpretations of Scripture passages in this chapter.

Chapter Four

Worshiping with Words

*The heavens declare the glory of God; the skies proclaim
the work of his hands.
Day after day they pour forth speech; night after night they
display knowledge.
There is no speech or language where their voice is not heard.
Their voice goes out into all the earth; and their words to
the ends of the world.*

Psalm 19:1-4a

In virtually any religious denomination it would be all but impossible to imagine a worship service that used no words. How else could we communicate with God and one another with precision? We cannot conceive of any other means whereby the details of human thought could be communicated, or for that matter, could even occur in our own minds. In the words of Henry Ward Beecher, the influential eighteenth century preacher and orator, "Thinking cannot be clear till it has had expression. We must write, or speak, or act our thoughts, or they will remain in a half torpid form."[1]

The left hemisphere of our brains contains most (but not all) of our verbal processing centers. What are the implications for worship when the primary element in our corporate worship experiences, verbalization, seems focused on one hemisphere of the brain? In what ways can words engage our right hemispheres, and how can we achieve the balance God intends? Let us now explore these issues.

How Does the Bible Talk about Worship?

Several Greek and Hebrew words in Scripture are translated as "worship" in English Bibles. Each word sheds its own light on how worship was perceived in that particular age and culture.

Prostration

The most frequently used Hebrew word translated as "worship" in English is *shachah* (shaw-KHAW). Its root meaning conveys the idea of prostration to royalty or a deity.[2] To judge from pictures surviving from ancient Egypt and Asia, such prostration is more than the gracious bowing before a modern monarch. *Shachah* would seem to indicate bowing with one's face touching the ground or even a full prostration, lying prone. This word is used frequently throughout the entire Old Testament.

The word itself paints a particularly vivid picture. For an ancient Hebrew to simply say the word *shachah* would conjure up a visual picture (right-brain) and excite the imagination (right-brain again) of what it would feel like to lie prone, nose in the dirt, utterly vulnerable, before a powerful, intimidating person. We should also note that to be prostrate is in most cases not a positive, uplifting experience. It implies self-abasement, even surrender. Right from the start we are confronted with an image for biblical worship that runs counter to today's positive, bright, and uplifting worship styles.

To simply say *shachah* is to be reminded of why one would fall prostrate before God. *Shachah* is not just the prostration of a mortal before an immortal. It is the abject surrender of a sinful mortal before a holy and righteous Immortal. There is in *shachah* the same dynamic that so often prompts angels when they appear to humankind to preface their address with the words "Fear not!" Why is fear the typical human response to the visitation of an angel? True, the supernatural can be scary, but beyond that is the sudden, jarring realization of sin that naturally accompanies a sudden encounter with utter purity. *Shachah* describes Isaiah's posture when he had his vision of God's throne (Isa. 6:5). He did not say, "Wow! I've always wanted to see what heaven would be like!" He said, "Woe is me! I am ruined!" We remember Jesus's words to Nicodemus (John 3:19, 20), "This is the verdict: Light has come into the world, but men loved darkness instead of light because their deeds were evil. Everyone who does evil hates the light, and will not come into the light for fear that his deeds will be exposed." *Shachah* describes the attitude of those who know who they are and who God is.

Prostration of one's heart and life is a true act of worship, but it is not always fun or uplifting. Yet all that is truly uplifting and joyful in worship can genuinely spring forth only from a heart that has first been face down before the Creator. But prostration is not just an Old Testament worship concept. In its Greek form, *proskuneo*, it is also the most common New Testament word for worship. And again, the word carries all the humbling characteristics of the Hebrew form. *Proskuneo* carries such meanings as "to fawn" or "to crouch." It is the word used for a dog licking the hand of its master.[3]

Prostration is the central biblical concept for worship. We cannot have biblical worship without it. But we cannot stop here. What of all the psalms urging us to "serve the Lord with gladness, come into his presence with singing?" Such psalms are the songs of the redeemed, the songs of self-acknowledged sinners who have been forgiven and raised to newness of life—abundant life. These are the songs of those who know the depths from which they have been saved. Perhaps some who complain that worship is dull feel that way because they have not yet confronted the depth of their own sin; thus they have no real sense of having been dramatically saved; and thus they have nothing profound to celebrate. To be fully aware of this degree of salvation is to be profoundly grateful, and such gratitude infuses worship with rich meaning. Such thankfulness naturally elicits in people a desire to serve the One who has redeemed them and given them such new life. And that brings us to our next key word for worship.

Service

Just as with "prostration," the second most common word translated in Scripture as worship, "service," is found in both the Old and New Testaments. "*Serve* the Lord with gladness" (Ps. 100:2 KJV); "When thou hast brought forth the people out of Egypt, ye shall *serve* God upon this mountain" (Exod. 3:12 KJV). At least, that's what we read in the King James Version of the Bible. Newer translations often translate the Hebrew *abad* as "worship," rather than "serve." *Abad* is used in quite a few different but related senses, but its basic meaning is "to work." Secondary meanings include "to serve, to till the ground, to enslave, to compel, to bring to pass"

and many more. Most often, *abad* is the Hebrew word translated "to serve" in the phrase "to serve the Lord."[4]

This word invites us to consider a much broader context for worship. A study of *abad* reveals that in the Hebrew mind-set, worship was indeed something one did by performing such religious acts as offering sacrifices, praying, praising, and the like. But well beyond these things, serving the Lord was an all-encompassing life vocation. One served the Lord while harvesting crops, cleaning the house, or disciplining the children. Worship was a way of living, a minute-by-minute attitude of the heart. Thus, another general principle about worship comes to the surface. All my life I have heard complaints that worship is often dull or boring. But when we make even the daily, mundane routines of life into acts of worship, our corporate worship is no longer an activity isolated from the rest of our lives. This vital connection with the "real world" can go far in adding relevance and luster to a Sunday service.

So the question arises: what would a service of worship look like in twenty-first century North America if it were truly holistic, if it reflected these biblical understandings of worship and appealed to all parts of the human brain?

It seems to me that the idea of prostration suggests a worship format that allows plenty of time for reflection upon who God is and who we are. Some denominations regularly include kneeling as part of the worship service—especially during confession and communion. We see now just how biblically based such actions are. Perhaps more worship traditions should consider including kneeling in their services.

But there are other ways to gain a fuller concept of God. Ample opportunities should be provided to prostrate the heart, whether or not the body actually follows suit. In my worship tradition, for example, there is an opening call to worship, an opening hymn, and a confession of sins, all of which is over in five or six minutes. I often question whether this interval provides enough time for people who have just arrived at worship to properly refocus their minds. Some other traditions have a lengthy period of singing and prayer at the beginning of worship. I believe such extended times of song and prayer can give people the time needed to redirect their

minds from such real but lesser concerns as getting the family out of bed, dressed, in the car, and to the church on time.

Interpretive dance, visual projections on a screen, and seasonal banners can all, when used with integrity, help instill a sense of humbleness before a holy God as evocative as the imagery of the Hebrew and Greek words for prostration themselves.

Insights arising from prostration certainly would also indicate that each service of worship should provide opportunity for corporate and personal confession followed by a joyful affirmation of forgiveness.

The biblical words for worship that carry the meaning of service remind us of the various communal aspects of worship. I am intrigued by the German word for worship, *Gottesdienst*, which means, simply, *the service of God*. But the term is ambiguous— does it refer to God's service to us or ours to God? Perhaps it refers to both, since worship is indeed a reciprocal event in which the ministries of service run both ways—and from one human to the others as well.

But we are often tempted to forget that worship is about service, even though we call it a "worship service." There is so much in our modern consumer-driven culture that prompts us to approach worship, instead, as we approach shopping. We expect a reward for our expenditure of time in worship, and if we fail to get the reward we're looking for, we'll shop around for another church that offers a better deal. This attitude is confirmed for me each time I hear a person utter that well-worn excuse for not going to church—"I don't get anything out of it." This mind-set fools us into thinking that worship is really about us and about getting our needs met. The biblical language about service corrects our self-centered worship habits, encouraging us, rather, to consider in worship how we might meet the needs of others during that very service and throughout the coming week.

Even a relatively small percentage of churchgoers committed to this sort of other-directed service in worship could revolutionize a congregation virtually overnight. I am not suggesting a particular right- or left-brain connection to these observations about service, but I do feel these are still points well worth making.

The Word of God

A central element of worship in virtually any Christian worship setting is the proclamation of the Word of God. But what exactly do we mean by the Word of God?

One of my more vivid and formative memories of childhood Sunday school is of a dear saint of a lady standing in front of our small junior-high class declaring that the only solid ground on which to build one's life (and here she raised high and shook her well-worn Bible) was "the Word of God." Ruth Ryland seemed rather old to us and not very imposing, with a sagging body and a rather high-pitched squeaky voice. But there was fire in her eyes and a look of fierce determination on her face as she proclaimed her credo. In that instant, this insubstantial old woman was transformed before my eyes into a formidable warrior for God.

It was through such simple childhood experiences that I learned to trust God and to believe his Word. And in that environment it was clearly communicated to me that "the Word of God" referred to the Bible. It never occurred to me that the term could have broader meanings. Later on, I became aware that when the biblical writers used the term "Word of God," they were generally not referring to the written Scriptures per se, but to the actual words God said—the things God chose to communicate—whether through prophet, priest, or king. And later still I learned from the first chapter of the Gospel of John that Jesus Christ, not the Bible, is the ultimate, the most complete "Word of God."

But what are we to make of such passages as Psalm 19—"The heavens *declare* the glory of God; the skies *proclaim* the work of his hands?" Is this yet another broadening of the meaning of "God's Word?" In what sense can the heavens themselves be considered the "Word of God?" The Hebrew in these opening verses is rather vague, as can be seen by contrasting various English translations, especially of verse 3. The New International Version says, "There is no speech or language where their [the heavens'] voice is not heard," implying both that the voice of the heavens can be heard among every language group of the earth and also that the voice is not only heard but also understood. The King James Version says

about the same thing. The New Revised Standard Version and the New American Standard Bible say, "There is no speech, nor are there words; their voice is not heard. . . ." This rendering suggests that even though one cannot actually hear the heavens with one's natural ears, "yet their voice goes out through all the earth." (Ps. 19:4a NRSV). Either way, it must be noted that the heavens, and by extension all of nature, are *proclaiming* God's glory on a global, even cosmic scale. This proclamation is clearly nonverbal communication and, in the specific case of the heavens, it is visual, right-brained, nonverbal communication. To the extent that a sovereign God chooses to speak through this part of his creation, he does. And if God speaks, what else can we call that speech but the Word of God?

This rather left-brained logic draws us to the conclusion that if God speaks to us through right-brained visual imagery, such as the heavens, that visual imagery then can be considered God's Word. The same might be said of such right-brain nonverbal forms of communication as a piece of music, the picture or symbol in a stained-glass window, or the expression on the face of a friend. To the extent that God's Spirit chooses to speak through these, to that extent they propound God's Word. If God has deigned to speak through Balaam's donkey (Num. 22), then it seems that God could speak through anything else in creation.

Given the variety of ways "God's Word" might be spoken, what does it mean to "proclaim God's Word" in worship? First, any time the Scriptures are read, God's Word is surely proclaimed. Comparing the amount of worship time spent reading the Scriptures versus the time spent delivering a sermon (and often the amount of time a minister spends preparing Scripture readings) one might easily conclude that the sermon is more important than the Scripture lessons upon which it is based. But surely the Scriptures are at least as important as our commentary upon them, no matter how inspired.

A well-constructed service might include numerous proclamations of God's Word, even if no sermon has been preached. Over the many years I have served churches as a minister of music, I have often found myself discussing whether a choir musical presentation might replace a sermon at a Sunday morning worship service. The point of discussion was always the same: is it possible

to say that the Word of God has been proclaimed if there has been no sermon in a worship service? If the preceding analysis about the Word of God is correct, the answer must be yes it is possible—but not guaranteed.

Second, many (but not all) hymns are in fact mini sermons and do precisely what sermons do—teach, exhort, evangelize, or admonish. The process of writing a well-crafted hymn text is surprisingly similar to writing a sermon. I know—I have attempted both! And it is interesting to note that the majority of hymn-text writers whose work is included in *The Presbyterian Hymnal* (1990) are ordained ministers. In either a sermon or a hymn, a section of Scripture is explored, or a theological subject is expounded in the light of Scripture. The difference, of course, is in the comparative length of each and in the fact that the hymn writer must submit to the added discipline of making the sermon into a poem. So if spoken sermons qualify as a proclamation of the Word of God, so do sung ones. Therefore I have maintained that a worship service featuring a well-chosen choral cantata or a hymn festival would not necessarily need to include a spoken sermon to proclaim the gospel sufficiently. And, as has been proposed above, in any service God will be speaking through many other venues as well, some of which use no words at all.

Checks and Balances

It is marvelous to observe how by God's design verbal and nonverbal forms of communication enrich each other. Right-brained, nonverbal speech can sometimes communicate more effectively than words, and sometimes not. We all know that there is a time to say, "I love you," and there are times when words will fall short and actually get in the way. Our loved one may even say, "Stop talking and give me a hug!" There are many times, however, when nonverbal communication lacks the necessary precision. Our loved one might then say, "What is *that* look supposed to mean?"

Because of this potential for imprecision and misunderstanding, I am not surprised that many times I have heard ministers and other church leaders express skepticism about the inclusion of non-

verbal elements in a worship service. That poem, musical selection, procession, or interpretive dance may be considered too open to various interpretations—or to no interpretation at all. But we cannot overrule God's design. God does at times address us nonverbally and opens the door for us to do the same even in worship.

Fortunately, we do not need to put full confidence in these nonverbal "words" alone. Historic Christianity has always rightly affirmed that since the ascension of Christ, who is the Word made Flesh, the written Word of God, the Bible, remains our primary and essential source for God's Word. God's nonverbal Word will always conform to the written Word. The first line of action for any who believe that God has spoken to them is to seek confirmation through the written word of sacred Scripture. Should biblical teaching in any way contradict the "word" one believes has come from God, that discrepancy should be enough to persuade the person that it was not God who spoke. Of course, many times it is not clear from Scripture whether God is speaking to us about a certain matter or not. In these situations, a second check is available to us; much prayer and counsel must be sought before acting. (Indeed, history is filled with the horrors done by those fully convinced that they were acting on God's orders.) Yet, as I have said, we cannot deny that God directly addresses us nonverbally simply because we're afraid that God may be misunderstood and untold damage done. When we ignore God's nonverbal, right-brain communications, or disallow them in our worship, we, in effect, muzzle the Spirit. It takes a whole brain to hear God's whole Word. We were created for fellowship (communication) with God and with each other. What a joy to hear God's voice and that of our neighbors in all the rich variety of ways the Lord has provided us!

When Words Mean More than Words

As we are seeing, God's communications regularly engage both hemispheres of our brain. Even within the world of words alone, however, we find plenty to engage the whole brain. The content, the logic, and the ideas of words speak to the left brain. Rich imagery

and symbolism, like that found especially (although certainly not exclusively) in poetry, tantalize the right brain.

What is it that drives the writers of poems and songs? Why not just get on with it and say what you want to say straight out and simply? We all know the answer. There are occasions—lots of them—when the only words we can think of seem inadequate. They just don't get to that place in our hearts that screams for expression. This is where the poet comes in. There is something about the rhythm and rhyme, the lilting sounds of well-chosen words, the power of simile and metaphor, that multiplies the intensity and levels of meaning. The poem says more than the sum of the words. We cannot explain the poem's effect on us because there are no words for it. It is not that we cannot *find* the words; there *are* no words. That is why there have always been and always will be poets. We need them. The poem gets to places in our brains where words in prose quite literally cannot go. God made us—and words—that way.

But even ordinary speech can take on many of the characteristics of poetry. That is one of the joys of reading great literature. We are not reading just to follow the story or plot; we enjoy a writer's turn of phrase and revel in the leanness or eloquence of the writing style. That is why so many find much pleasure in reading and re-reading such authors as Ernest Hemingway, James Michener, J. R. R. Tolkien, C. S. Lewis, or Flannery O'Connor. Each has a unique and engaging way of using the English language.

The multiplicity of Bible translations available today is a source of both benefits and problems in relation to right-brain/left-brain matters. It is helpful to know which translations serve best for certain situations. Some versions of Scripture are especially appropriate for various reading levels, cultural groups, or study needs. Some translations strive so hard for a faithful, literal translation of the original languages that the resulting English has a stiff, awkward feel; it doesn't flow. Such translations may be great for study purposes, but the narrative passages lose their intrigue and charm, and the poetic books such as the Psalms or Song of Solomon have every drop of lyricism drained out. They, in fact, cease to be truly poetic books. All of these factors obviously have direct bearing on our discussion of right-brain/left-brain issues in worship. The left brain will be offended if the translation is not accurate (assuming that

anyone notices). The right brain will be offended if the literary style of the translation spoils the biblical poetry or story. On the other hand, doing Bible study with multiple texts before us can shed much light as both sides of the brain are more fully engaged.

Well-crafted language has ramifications for all aspects of the spoken word in worship—sermons, prayers, even announcements. Some speakers are simply more engaging than others. Although I was taught in childhood and youth that "real" prayers are always extemporaneous, I have learned to value the use of published prayers in leading public worship. There is a lot to be said for having just the right words in just the right sequence at just the right time. "A word fitly spoken is like apples of gold in pictures of silver" (Prov. 25:11 KJV). If you were leading a delegation of representatives from your state in presenting a petition to the president of the United States, you would take immense care to prepare your remarks. Worship leaders should make at least as much careful preparation in presenting the church's petitions before the sovereign ruler of the universe.

I have noticed over the years that quite a few worship leaders, regardless of denomination, make use of the *Book of Common Prayer* of the Episcopal Church. I know of no worship resource that is more biblically rich, incisive, and filled with beautiful prose. There is no stuttering, no needless repetition, no break in the flow of logic, no going off on tangents. The language is lean and to the point. Every word is laden with meaning; the loss of any single word would seriously detract from the fullness of the thought. It is truly a case in which less is more. But beyond all this, the language is simply beautiful. It is not poetry, but it feels as though it were. As with any great literature, the very hearing of it is both healing and salutary. I know of no finer example of both high theology and soaring lyricism, of reasoned thought and fertile imagination, of right and left brains working together than the *Book of Common Prayer*. I frequently use this resource when I am asked to offer prayer in worship settings. It is remarkable how often people ask me for copies of my prayer. They seem to notice the difference and find themselves moved to more profound levels of prayer than they usually experience in their regular worship services. They are hungry for more, so they ask for a copy of the prayer. This experience is

for me further confirmation of the way God blesses words "fitly spoken."

Moving beyond Words

Words are indeed marvelous things. By them we come to know ourselves, each other, and our God, who comes to us as the Word made Flesh. We have seen how words, though largely processed in the left brain, are laden with right-brain associations as well. Many of the words we use in worship are not merely spoken, however. They are sung. What happens in our brains when we further enrich our poetic words with language of music? That is our next topic for consideration.

Questions for Thought and Discussion

1. Discuss your definition of worship prior to reading this chapter and your thoughts since reading this chapter.
2. What is God's Word? Discuss your thoughts as you read the suggestions in this chapter that the *meaning* of God's Word may be conveyed in more ways than the written account.
3. In the formal worship service, is the proclaiming of God's Word accomplished solely by preaching? Why do you answer as you do?
4. To what extent is nonverbal proclamation a viable and valuable means of making God's Word known?
5. Discuss any other means of worship that might help people to serve God with their hearts, souls, and minds.

Chapter Five

Songs, Sacraments, and Symbols

Those who sing pray twice.

—Augustine of Hippo

Songs, sacraments, and symbols are united by more than the fact that they all begin with the same letter. They are the three most common forms of nonverbal communication in most services of Christian worship. We will explore each in turn, showing how they are all central to worship and largely right-brained in orientation.

Music In Worship

In the previous chapter we spoke of the ways various forms of verbalization add levels of meaning that go beyond the words themselves. Now, if we take those supercharged words we call a poem, or even prose fitly spoken, and set them to beautiful or at least appropriate music, we are elevated to even higher levels of nonverbal communication. Now even more information is being profoundly expressed that words, even poetic words, literally cannot say.

Many years ago a woman came up to me after a Sunday communion service. I could tell by the intent look in her eyes that she had something serious to say. "Bob, that organ music you played during communion today . . . it was . . . it was . . . well, it was like a second sermon! Thank you. Thank you!" Her struggle for words was understandable and exactly to the point. She was trying to use words to describe something for which there were no words. I knew better than to ask her what that second sermon was about.

Music has historically been honored in Christian worship for its ability to interpret and add levels of meaning to words. But if all we have been saying about nonverbal communication is valid, then the music itself, apart from any words, can stand as a God-ordained vehicle of communication. Then a piece of music that has no connection to any words whatsoever might still be God's vehicle for dialogue with us. I am proposing that God created music from the beginning not merely as a form of entertainment but as a means for communication—a sort of communication different from verbal speech and supplementary to it. For all of Augustine's worry that music sometimes distracted him from the meaning of the words, he seems nonetheless to have had some understanding of music as a separate form of communication. His much-quoted phrase "Those who sing pray twice" reveals his grasp of music as a powerful and useful language quite distinct from words. Yet this line of thinking is exceedingly rare among Christian thinkers. Jerome goes so far as to counsel a mother that her daughter "be deaf to the sound of the organ, and not know even the uses of the pipe, the lyre, and the cithara."[1]

The twentieth century German theologian Dietrich Bonhoeffer shares this perception:

All devotion, all attention should be concentrated upon the Word in the hymn. . . . [W]e do not hum a melody; we sing words of praise to God, words of thanksgiving, confession and prayer. Thus the music is completely the servant of the Word.[2]

As we shall see in in chapter 6, the Puritan tradition vigorously embraced this line of thinking. The following warning is typical:

Cautions are necessary with respect to Musick and Painting; the fancy is often too quick in them, and the Soul too much affected by the Senses. . . . Should Christians squander away so many precious Hours in Vanity, or take Pleasure in gratifying a Sense that has so often been a Traitor to Virtue?[3]

One catches in all these voices a sort of love-hate relationship with music. Its beauty and benefits cannot be denied, yet we find

throughout history this sense of caution about those very beauties and benefits—a skepticism that seems to say, "Anything that good has got to be bad for you."

But in its best moments the church of Jesus Christ has known that such asceticism, such opposition to some of God's best gifts, has no true home in the Christian tradition. On this fallen planet, where there is a gift of God, there is a perversion and misuse of that gift as well. To run away from God's good gifts because they are often misused is at best an abdication of our responsibilities to be good stewards of all that God gave us and, at worst, a blasphemy against the God who gave those gifts. Christians are called not to surrender to the world's perversions, but to join Christ in acts of redemption of a twisted and broken world. Fully aware of our own potential, even our predilection to such distortion, we are still called to be examples of a fuller, richer, redeemed humanity. The church should exhibit the fullest possible manifestation of redeemed humanity and a redeemed world.

Steven Guthrie, professor of theology at St. Andrews University, Scotland, observes that the apostle Paul's attitude about music differs from that of the authors cited above. Basing his argument on Paul's Letter to the Ephesians, he interprets Paul's injunction that Christians are to "speak to one another with psalms, hymns, and spiritual songs" (Eph. 5:19) as a charge for Christians to come out of the darkness of their old lives and to live as children of the light. Guthrie writes:

> To a Christian community surrounded by ignorance and immorality; to a people who were themselves prone to the blindness and indulgence of their former way of life; at the conclusion of a passage warning against irrationality and sins of the flesh—Paul urges singing and music making.
>
> The contrast with the first passages we considered [quotations from Augustine, Calvin, Athanasius, and Bonhoeffer, some of which are cited above] could not be more stark. Paul shares the same broad concerns as Augustine and Calvin, but the recommendation emerging from those concerns is entirely different. To put it very crudely, Augustine says: "Irrationality is bad. Sensuality is bad. Therefore, be careful about music." Paul on the other

hand says, "Foolishness is bad. Sensuality is bad. Therefore, you had better sing."[4]

Why did God create music and the other arts? It was not just for our enjoyment, not just for our recreation, though even if this were the case, it would be reason enough for their full incorporation in Christian life and worship. But they were created also because in God's grand scheme of things, God has all manner of things to say that words cannot say. That was his plan before the foundation of the world. That is why he designed our brains as he did. And when God saw all that he had made, behold, it was very good.

But music and the other arts are not good at everything. These right-brained ways of communicating are essential, but they are not the sorts of mental processes that can provide a clear line of logical thought. For that we need the left brain. And I emphasize the word *need*. For while the right brain feeds the world of imagination and aesthetics, the left brain is the domain of facts, figures, and reason. It is the guardian of propositional truth, whether theological, scientific, or rational in general. How can we be sure that the essential but murky right brain is sending messages that are good and true? Our left brain cross-references them in light of the clear, hard rigors of logic and rationality. The fact that God has much to say that transcends the world of words is not to diminish the absolute necessity of words. The Bible may not be the only way God speaks, but it is the Word of God in the most concrete form we have. And the church has traditionally affirmed that it is the duty and delight of all Christians to conform their lives to the Word of God as fully as possible. If we may be guilty of shortchanging God's intentions by limiting right-brained elements in worship and life—and many of us are—there is far greater danger if we shortchange the left-brained elements. The reformers were dead right about that. There is far greater danger in shortchanging left-brain elements because God's attributes and will for us are made known primarily in rational discourse. If you really want to know *details* about your redemption, the Holy Spirit, or the life to come, studying Calvin's *Institutes* or Luther's *Augsburg Confession* will get you further than listening to Bach's "Jesu, Joy of Man's Desiring"

or meditating on Michelangelo's *The Creation* in the Sistine Chapel. The whole point of this book, after all, is to show that certain parts of the brain are better than others at certain tasks. Music can sometimes do what words cannot; words can sometimes do what music cannot. It's all about balance.

The Sacraments

Just as music engages the right hemisphere of the average worshiper, so does the symbolism of the sacraments. Augustine of Hippo crystallized the definition of sacraments into "a visible sign of an invisible grace."[5] A sign is something that points to something else, and sacraments certainly do that. The bread points to Christ's body, the wine to his blood. But sacraments are also symbols, which is a slightly different matter. Symbols do more than merely point to something else; they *represent* the object to which they refer. They represent by some sort of resemblance.[6] Red wine resembles blood. Bread can be torn and broken, just as the body of Christ was. Jesus's words, "This is my body, this is my blood," lie at the heart of the meaning of the Eucharist. Christians differ as to whether these words are merely symbolic or more than symbolic, but all agree they are *at least* symbolic. For many Christians, "This is my body" is metaphoric language, in which one thing is said to be another thing, as in Luther's famous hymn "A Mighty Fortress Is Our God." Jesus's metaphoric words invite us to imagine the ways the bread might symbolize his body. Bread can be broken, it nourishes those who take it in, and it must "come through the fire." As the individual grains of wheat are crushed and broken to become one loaf, so the individual Christian is called to die to self to become part of the one Body of Christ. As the sacraments embody this sort of symbolism and creative imagination, they stimulate the right side of the brain. And they are remarkably efficient! One who has come to understand the various meanings of a symbol can grasp in an instant what would take hours to propound fully with words.

For Christians who hold that there is more than mere symbolism occurring at the eucharistic meal, there is even further right-brain stimulation. The various eucharistic theologies of real presence,

consubstantiation, and transubstantiation all further engage our imaginations as we seek understanding of these mysteries.

And so we see some ways that symbols can speak. In many Christian traditions, not only the sermon but the sacraments as well are considered to be a proclamation of the Word. R. J. Gore, Jr., professor of systematic theology at Erskine Theological Seminary, writes, "Calvin viewed the Word as more extensive than the sermon. Indeed, borrowing from Augustine, he spoke of the Lord's Supper as a 'visible word.' Thus, in understanding Calvin's thinking, it is a grave error to replace the primacy of the Word with the primacy of preaching."[7] Gore means for us to see that Calvin's emphasis on the primacy of the Word in worship includes the sacraments. They too, and not just the sermon, are a proclamation of the Word. As Calvin himself states, "For, that the Word may not beat your ears in vain, and that the sacraments may not strike your eyes [we might add, your nose, taste, and touch] in vain, the Spirit shows us that in them *it is God speaking to us*"[8] (italics added).

"Word and Sacrament" is a phrase much used to summarize the chief functions of the clergy in a service of worship. They preach the Word and administer the sacraments. Once again we see the marvelous balance between right- and left-brain functions. But again we must be careful not to oversimplify the distinction. Preaching can appeal to the right brain through the use of symbolism or various illustrations. But it is a verbal enterprise by definition, and therefore largely left-brained. In the same way the sacraments focus on right-brain symbolism and visualization. Yet no sacrament can be rightly administered without the use of words.

There are actually too *few* words in most Protestant Communion celebrations. A study of the suggested communion liturgies provided by most mainline denominations reveals a much lengthier prayer prior to distribution than many pastors tend to use. This Prayer of Thanksgiving is based on ancient models. Communion is often called Eucharist, which simply means "thanksgiving." When this great trinitarian prayer is eliminated or truncated, as is so often the case, we severely limit the congregation's opportunity to perform one of the central functions of the sacrament—to remember all that God has done in the past in Jesus Christ, and the sure promise to bring in the kingdom in all its fullness—to remember all

this and to *give thanks*! It is as if we want to get through all this as quickly as we can. After all, the service must be over in an hour! Right-brained symbols can speak eloquently, but for them to speak efficiently and truthfully, they need to be properly understood. The Eucharist is central to Christian worship, but many people are not sure what they are to focus their minds upon during the sacrament. Many thoughts are appropriate for communion, but not just any thoughts. The full eucharistic prayer is an instance in which a bit more left-brained verbal guidance can truly help the right brain apprehend the symbolism in more depth and keep it theologically sound. What marvelous cooperation between the hemispheres is afforded in this sacrament!

Sign Value

Another issue related to the way communion is celebrated is what James F. White, professor of liturgical studies at Drew University, calls sign value—how well do the objects and actions of our celebration signify the true meaning of the sacrament?[9] The waters of baptism speak of the complete cleansing from all our sin, our plunging into the death of Christ and our being raised into newness of life, and the massive waters of Noah's flood.[10] A slight moistening of one's forehead with one dab of water can never portray all of that. A minister should at least take a good handful of water so that all present not only see but also hear the water. I wonder why many congregations so often settle for a single application of water when the earliest records we have instruct three applications of water as the trinitarian formula is pronounced.[11] It is as if we are ashamed of the waters of baptism. Often the sign value of our sacraments as we practice them is counterproductive in that it reinforces a message different from our sacramental theologies. Further, I have heard ministers give extended commentary during a sacrament that had the effect of a second sermon. Here again, the sign value can easily get lost in the sea of verbiage, especially if the symbolism is being underplayed. (The issue is not the words per se, but the relative importance of words to the sacred actions and elements.)

Sign value is an issue with the sacrament of Holy Communion as well. If Christ's body is represented as one loaf in Scripture, and

the breaking of that loaf as our participation in the broken body of Christ, and if that one loaf also speaks of how we who are many are made one body as we partake of the one loaf,[12] would not the best sign be to use one loaf of bread in our communion services? Why do so many Christian congregations disregard the importance of Paul's teaching by downplaying the loaf and partaking of tiny individual wafers or bread cubes? The symbolism of these individual servings of bread seems to run exactly counter to Paul's teaching in 1 Corinthians. It is counterproductive to promulgate a symbol that seems to teach individualism rather than oneness with Christ and his church. The sign value is inappropriate not just because of the loss of the one loaf, but because the servings tend to be minuscule. These miniature servings do not communicate the massiveness of God's love and grace as seen in the life, death, and resurrection of Jesus Christ.

Another issue related to the sign value of the Lord's Supper has to do with frequency of celebration. How often should a congregation celebrate the Eucharist? Most churches agree that the older tradition of quarterly celebrations was too infrequent. Annual informal surveys that I do in my seminary worship classes show that across a wide variety of denominations, the majority of churches have drastically increased the frequency of the sacrament from the earlier quarterly practice. That is a move in the right direction. But increasingly, as I study the Scriptures on this subject, I am convinced that there is direct biblical evidence in support of weekly (if not daily) celebrations of the Eucharist. We know that during the years the New Testament was being written, the embryonic Christian community had already decided to establish the first day of the week (Sunday) rather than the Sabbath (Saturday) as their main meeting day,[13] and that this became known as "the Lord's Day."[14] We read in Acts 20:7, "On the first day of the week we came together to break bread." This verse bears witness to two things— the meeting day was Sunday, and the reason for the meeting was "to break bread." There are 12 occurrences of the term "break bread" in the New Testament.[15] Five of these references are accounts of the Last Supper. Actually, there are seven references if one includes the Emmaus account in Luke 24, which I and others view as a teaching about eucharistic gatherings.

Further, we have a curious repetition of ideas about meals in Acts 2. This passage, which also contains the Pentecost account, is the primal account of life in the Christian community. We are told in verse 42 that the Christians devoted themselves to four things—the apostles' teaching, the fellowship, the breaking of bread, and prayer. What is meant by "the breaking of bread?" Is this a reference merely to eating meals together or a direct reference to the Lord's Supper? Then in verse 46, we are told again that "They broke bread in their homes," but this time Luke adds, "and [they] ate together with glad and sincere hearts." What is meant by this repetition of breaking bread together *and* eating together? Is there a difference between breaking bread and eating together? We cannot know for sure. If it were an example of Hebrew poetry, we might say this is merely a case of poetic parallelism. But this is clearly not a poetic passage. Is Paul just outlining the events of a meal, saying in effect, "You have to break the bread before you can eat it"? It could be, but it seems unlike Paul to make such a trivial observation. The most logical interpretation would seem to be that Paul was describing two events—a communal meal similar to our covered-dish dinners, and the Lord's Supper.

There is much evidence that the New Testament church's communion celebrations took place within the context of a full meal called an Agape Feast. At a given point in the meal, the leader would call for the group's attention, deliver a sermon or address, and distribute the bread and cup.[16] It would appear that this is the custom referred to by Paul in 1 Corinthians 11:

> In the following directives I have no praise for you, for your meetings do more harm than good. In the first place, I hear that when you come together as a church, there are divisions among you, and to some extent I believe it. No doubt there have to be differences among you to show which of you have God's approval. When you come together, it is not the Lord's Supper you eat, for as you eat, each of you goes ahead without waiting for anybody else. One remains hungry, another gets drunk. Don't you have homes to eat and drink in? Or do you despise the church of God and humiliate those who have nothing? What shall I say to you? Shall I praise you for this? Certainly not! [vv. 17-22].

How could one get drunk simply by passing the communion cup around? There appears to be a whole lot more eating here too than a Eucharist would entail. Some remain hungry, because others are eating without waiting for everyone to arrive. This does not sound like a mere communion celebration. It is, in fact, what the early church called an Agape Meal, a Love Feast. It seems that Paul was not keen on the idea of these meals from the start. "Don't you have homes to eat and drink in?" he scolds. I do not think this means that Paul was against church dinners, but he seems to oppose including a eucharistic celebration as part of them. It is also important to note that Paul's language suggests that *each* of their "meetings" (1 Cor. 11:17, 20) includes the Eucharist.

We also have the witness of the *Didache*, the earliest post–New Testament document that gives instruction about Christian worship. In chapter 14 we read, "But every Lord's day gather yourselves together, and break bread, and give thanksgiving. . . ."[17] This document, dating from about the year A.D. 100, gives clear evidence of the eucharistic character of the Lord's Day assemblies in that time and place. Then the First Apology of Justin Martyr, written in Rome in about A.D. 150, states in a chapter on "The Weekly Meetings of the Christians," that these meetings consisted of readings of the apostles and prophets, instruction by the president, prayers, and a distribution of the bread and wine to each.[18]

Because of all this evidence, I can only assume that the New Testament Church met together frequently, perhaps every day (Acts 2:46), for the express purpose of breaking bread; that is, celebrating the Lord's Supper. If this analysis is correct, it is most interesting to consider that the New Testament gives no such extensive endorsement for preaching at every gathering. Of course, Scripture calls us to include preaching in worship as well (Gal. 1:8; 2 Tim. 4:2) But in the light of the evidence above, it is curious that Protestantism has insisted on weekly sermons—and lengthy ones at that—while the sacrament has often been relegated to a mere four times a year—or less. The New Testament seems simply to assume that if Christians met to worship, they celebrated the Lord's Supper.

It was the expressed desire of Luther, Calvin, Knox, and many of the Puritans, as well as Wesley, that the Lord's Supper be celebrated as frequently as possible. Calvin vainly pleaded with the

church authorities for weekly communion. Wesley said he would take the Eucharist every day if he could. Knox and many of the Puritans also favored very frequent communions. At least two things hindered Puritan efforts. First, the lack of ordained ministers made anything like regular celebrations impossible. But even where ministers were available, the reformers were often unsuccessful in persuading the people to attend regular communion services. After a lifetime of experience with a single communion celebration a year, usually at Easter, it was difficult to reprogram the thinking of the hard-headed Scots to accept truly frequent celebrations. Over time, the less-frequent scheduling of the sacrament became institutionalized and sadly, in many places, canonized. It is a great mystery to me how and why the infrequent celebration of the Lord's Supper has been allowed to go on for so long when the teaching of Scripture seems so clear on the subject. Fortunately, the well-established trend now is to reverse this long-neglected state of affairs. Yet, though many mainline denominations recommend weekly communion, most congregations are still far from the weekly celebrations of the New Testament church. We seem to insist upon spiritually starving ourselves.

This study of the centrality of the sacraments to Christian worship emphasizes once again the inherent right-brain/left-brain balance that biblical worship provides, or can provide, when the full diet of Word and Sacrament is present at each gathering of the faithful. I have gone to considerable lengths about the sacraments because I believe Scripture calls for weekly celebrations and because they offer us one of the best ways to achieve better balance in worship. If churches offer Holy Communion every month at the very least, and if it is celebrated with due consideration for proper sign value, the Word of God can be proclaimed with the richness and power God intends.

Sacramental Worship

The sacraments are liturgical acts that at the very least convey special meaning. But many other liturgical acts also convey meaning. They are not sacraments, but they are sacramental. In his book *Evangelicals on the Canterbury Trail: Why Evangelicals Are*

Attracted to the Liturgical Church, Robert Webber, professor of worship at Northern Seminary in Lombard, Illinois, provides a disarming account of his personal faith journey from fundamentalism through a circuitous route to the Episcopal Church. Much of the attraction of Anglicanism for him was related to the sacramental nature of this worship tradition. Sacramental worship is characterized first by its placing much emphasis on the sacraments. But beyond using simply water, wine, and bread, *sacramental acts* would include in addition to the sacraments other visible and tangible signs and acts through which one's "relationship with God in faith is established, repaired, and maintained."[19] Among these might be anointing with oil, foot washing, the laying on of hands, application of ashes on Ash Wednesday, and other symbolic acts. While Webber was drawn into such worship by a powerful longing to know Jesus more deeply, he found some compelling theological reasons to support his move:

> First, I've become sacramental because of the incarnation. I've always believed God became human. But not until ten years ago did I begin to wrestle with the implication of the incarnation. The incarnation affirmed that God became one of us. . . . The point, of course, is that God became present to his world not in a spiritual, bodiless, timeless, spaceless way. Rather, he became human in flesh and blood, in time, space, and history. The incarnation affirms that God acted through material creation to give us his salvation. Here then is the sacramental principle! God uses his created order as a vehicle of his saving, comforting, and healing presence.[20]

After expressing how his discovery of the early church fathers such as Cyprian, Augustine, Ambrose, Athanasius, and St. John Chrysostom enriched his life, he continues his discussion of sacramentality:

> I was surprised to discover that these fathers thought in terms of one sacrament—one visible, tangible means by which we are brought to God. That means is Jesus Christ. He is *the* sacrament *par excellence*. The fathers never argued for salvation by the sac-

raments. Rather, the sacraments of water and bread and wine, they said, are the visible, tangible signs of Christ's saving action. The purpose of the sacrament is to signify Christ and thus provide a sign of his encounter with us.

Consequently, the fathers saw many things as sacramental. They recognized many means by which Christ's saving reality was signified. Tertullian, for example, went back to the Old Testament and saw sacramental signs everywhere: the Exodus is sacramental because it points to the Christ event; the offices of prophet, priest, and king are sacramental because they are fulfilled in Christ. . . . Even the Tabernacle and the Temple, with all their sacrifices and sacred rituals, were seen as sacramental. What is important here is that all these visible, tangible, and concrete realities were shadows of what was to come. They looked to Jesus, the person whose reality they signified.

When the early fathers evaluated the New Testament church . . . they spoke not only of Baptism and the Lord's Supper as visible means by which we are brought to Christ, but also of the Gospels, prayer, the study of doctrine, and the power of a life led as a good example.

. . . I discovered that this sacramental sense is not as far removed from my Evangelical background as it first appeared. I had always believed the Scriptures somehow mysteriously represented the means through which God became present to the reader. All I had to do was extend this principle to all of life and to specific signs of God's acting in the church.[21]

A heightened awareness of these sacramental aspects of worship with all their symbolism, their visual and even tactile qualities, cannot help but engage the worshiping brain more fully. It remains for us now to explore the nature and power of symbolism itself in worship.

Symbolism

Symbolism is important to God and therefore should be taken seriously by us as well. Symbols are powerful indeed in our worship,

as in our everyday lives. For those with a mind-set of "the simpler, the better" about worship, the mere discussion of symbolism, let alone any manifestation of it, can be disturbing. I have observed this sense of distress in some in my worship classes as well as in various church committees when a suggestion about including some symbolic act or object was being discussed. Sometimes the concern is to avoid anything that might be considered "high church." I can still hear the immediate reaction of one of my older seminary students: "But I thought we [Protestants] were trying to get away from all that pomp." I have heard other ready objections for fear that the proposed addition might distract from worship or even encourage superstition! Yet one cannot avoid symbolism. Even the most simply designed worship room will feature multiple layers of symbolism. There may not be any stained glass, banners, paraments, candles, or even flowers; and the minister and choirs may just be wearing regular street clothes. But still there will be symbolism all around. The arrangement of the chairs or pews will be a symbol of the role the congregation is given in worship. If set in straight, parallel rows facing forward, they will symbolize the belief that the congregation is to focus its attention on what is happening up front. If the seating is designed with a gentle curve, this will speak of a desire for the congregation to see each other better, symbolizing the importance of the relationships among members of the congregation. If the chairs are set up so that the people face each other across a central aisle, the message of the importance of congregational community will be all the stronger. A business suit is as symbolic in its own way as a robe or other vestment, perhaps symbolizing that the pastor is one with the congregation. For that matter, even if worship leaders wear blue jeans and T-shirts, they are still engaging in high symbolism. Whatever clothing one wears, the style is associated with a particular segment of society. And a decision *not* to wear a liturgical robe may be seen as a decision not to separate one's self from the congregation, not to appear too haughty, or even as a sort of rebellion against authority.

What catches your eye upon entry into a worship room? Do you first notice a high central pulpit, symbolizing the centrality of the preached word? Do you first notice a large communion table given central place—a symbol of the preeminence of the Eucharist?

Perhaps you observe that pulpit, font, and table are placed such that all three receive equal status, thus symbolizing the equal status of Word and Sacrament. Whenever a worship space is built, someone has to make a decision about where to place these basic furnishings. And that chosen arrangement will thereafter stand as a living symbol of a theology of worship.

In many if not most church-building programs I have observed, an architect is engaged for the project, and perhaps some basic conversations take place about how to build the sanctuary. But because of limited congregational funds or church people's lack of knowledge about worship matters, or both, architects are often pretty much left to their own devices. Consequently, the architect simply designs a basic church, one that looks like so many other churches. I've seen this design over and over, all over the country in Methodist, Baptist, independent, Presbyterian, and Pentecostal churches: Fixed pews in even rows face straight forward, one central pulpit stands on a platform with the choir behind facing the congregation. A small table is placed directly in front of the pulpit. That's about it. Thus is lost a once-in-a-lifetime chance to really consider what worship is and what design might best facilitate that understanding. Yet, even when no one has recently given these matters much thought, someone in the past did. This architectural design is just one of many designs used throughout history. Such things do not just "happen." When most church designs were first conceived, they were in reaction to some previous design and changed for a particular reason. Meaning and purpose stood behind those decisions.

Beyond these issues of basic room design, symbolism can be seen in the furnishings used as well. As one looks around even a bare-bones worship space, one will probably note that somewhere, on the pulpit, communion table, or perhaps on a pew or on a door, a cross or other sacred design will have been etched, painted, or otherwise affixed. It is the rare church, indeed, that has no cross displayed anywhere. The very arrangement of the seats or perhaps the aisles is often in a cruciform design.

One cannot avoid symbolism, nor would we want to. Not just our buildings, but our human relationships are permeated with symbolic acts. Every time we shake hands, open the door for someone

else, offer a hug, salute the flag (or burn it), stand up during a worship service, or blow out our birthday candles, we enact a little ceremony—a ritual—that has symbolic meaning.

A recent controversy in South Carolina gives stark testimonial to the profound power of symbols in our everyday lives. Until July 2000 the Confederate battle flag had been flying atop the South Carolina State House in Columbia. For many, it was a symbol of Southern heritage and a way of honoring the many South Carolinians who died in the Civil War. For other South Carolinians it was a hated sign of racial oppression that had no business being flown on a government building in this day and age. The two sides argued past each other for years. Tensions mounted. Demonstrations were held. The NAACP imposed a boycott upon the entire state. Finally, after prolonged and agonizing debate, the state legislature voted to remove the Confederate battle flag from the top of the capitol dome. The compromise was to place it instead at the Confederate memorial site on the front lawn. Needless to say, for many opposed to the flag's presence anywhere on government property, this was still an unsatisfactory solution. For many on the other side, it was a sad day indeed when the flag was lowered from the capitol dome for the last time. This controversy remains a vivid and enduring reminder of how powerfully symbols can communicate.

This controversy also demonstrates how a symbol can communicate more than one thing. The cross was a symbol of punishment, shame, oppression, and torture. After the death of Jesus Christ, Christians added new meanings to this symbol, meanings that eventually superseded the old ones. The cross came to symbolize redemption, forgiveness, hope, and the power of divine love. Therefore, symbols need to be carefully, lovingly, and respectfully explained, so that all are clear about their meaning. A symbol that no one understands has no meaning at all. That's part of what John Calvin was reacting against. A symbol that comes to have conflicting meanings may well become divisive and destructive. But a symbol that is commonly understood and cherished is one of the most powerful and efficient forms of communication imaginable. Throughout history, people have given their lives for a symbol. Soldiers run to retrieve a flag dropped by a fallen comrade. Countless saints have martyred themselves for the sake of the cross. Husbands or wives know they are in big trouble if they lose their wedding

rings. Our churches are filled with symbols. Do we even know what they mean? Do we rehearse their meaning together as a community of faith, to avail ourselves of their inherent power?

Caution—Obstructions Ahead

Song, sacrament, and symbol stand as foundational elements of virtually all Christian worship. This is the Lord's design—the Lord who in both the Old and New Testaments instructs us to include them all. Churches that consistently do so have already made significant progress on the road to maintaining a healthy balance between right-brain and left-brain stimulation.

But the route is filled with roadblocks. Before we make our final observations and recommendations in chapter 9, we have numerous issues to consider. It will be wise to consider the practical hindrances that tend to frustrate the progress of many churches as they travel this road toward holistic worship. One such hindrance lies within the unique personality of any given Christian denomination. Each branch of the church exhibits characteristics that make it different from all the others. Can certain elements in a denominational personality be at the same time a strength and a weakness? That is the issue we explore in the next chapter.

Questions for Thought and Discussion

1. Think of music and visual imagery that you have experienced in corporate worship, and list those God has used to speak to you in nonverbal ways. How have these nonverbals enhanced your *knowing* God?
2. Think of your experiences participating in the Lord's Supper, and reflect on your prayers. Did the worship leader use words in such a way that your thoughts were engaged as you handled and tasted the wine and the bread? Were you verbalizing your prayers in your mind and heart, or were you struggling to focus upon their meaning?
3. Spend some time reading Scripture regarding early church practice. Discuss your faith tradition's practices regarding the Eucharist or Lord's Supper.

Chapter Six

Denominational Ethos

I have become all things to all people, that by all means I might save some.

—1 Corinthians 9:22b ESV

There is a certain "feel" to a denomination's worship and life. It has to do with the worship elements, the selections of music, the preaching style and content, and the degree of a congregation's active participation in the worship service. But there is much more to the "feel" than that. Theological ideologies, geographical-cultural conditionings, and socioeconomic factors all play large roles as well. We are talking about the *ethos* of the denomination—the personality of a group of people. Ethos is much the same as *culture,* though culture generally refers to a much broader area of concerns. Culture refers to the institutions, behaviors, arts, and beliefs of a people group. Ethos has more to do with the intuitive qualities that distinguish one group from another, the personality of a group. It has more to do with feelings and perceptions.

This *ethos* or personality may not be equally discernable in every congregation of a denomination, but for the most part it is a recognizable living thing not to be confused with the ethos of most other denominational traditions.

Denominational Personalities

Suppose a loyal Presbyterian goes with a friend to a Greek Orthodox Sunday service. The Presbyterian is used to sitting in church rather passively, singing a few hymns, praying a few prayers, and listening to a sermon lasting from 15 to 45 minutes, depending on the church. The hymns she sings are likely to expound on some

point of doctrine or to challenge one to higher levels of service. The sermon is a carefully reasoned exposition of a passage of Scripture designed to teach doctrine—or perhaps the sermon features the old three-points-and-a-poem format on how to deal with various life issues.

The Presbyterian is about to enter a whole new universe of meaning. The Orthodox service seems mystical and otherworldly. The room is filled with opulent sights and sounds and smells. People are kissing pictures, making the sign of the cross on their bodies, and standing for a long, long time. The priests' garments are of phenomenal workmanship. The Presbyterian notices that the service does not seem focused on the people and their needs; most of the words are to and about God. An English translation of the Greek is provided in the service book. Knowing the Bible pretty well, the visitor notices that practically every word is either a direct biblical quote or an allusion to something in Scripture. And virtually everything is sung, or at least chanted. Every act of the priests and the people seems to be filled with special meanings. Symbolism permeates the service. And overarching all is the sense that she is being translated into the heavens, into the very presence of God.

I do not present this contrast to recommend one worship service over the other. Frankly, both traditions could learn much from one another. One excels in learning *about* God and making practical applications to life situations. The other, when properly understood, excels in leading us into the presence of that God. And, of course, one is heavier on left-brained elements, and the other is more right-brained.

Our Presbyterian, by the way, might as easily have been taken to a nondenominational charismatic praise-and-worship service and have an encounter surprisingly similar to the one at the Greek Orthodox church. One of the great strengths of the charismatic style of worship is that it gives adequate time for worshipers to break with the myriad of thoughts racing through their minds and slowly to shift their focus to God. The whole philosophy behind this style is a conviction that one should first praise and then move into worship. In this understanding, the praise component consists of songs and prayers (but mostly songs) that praise God for what he has done for us. These songs tend to be upbeat and on the loud side.

Gradually, the worship leader moves the congregation from praise to the quieter pace of worship. This tradition understands worship to be a style of singing and praying that focuses on God merely for who he is, apart from what he has done for us. Worship songs tend to be reflective and infused with quiet awe.[1] The praise-and-worship tradition also often describes this sequence as a symbolic progression from the outer temple courts, moving gradually into the Holy of Holies. Churches in this tradition tend to place great value on the importance of music with many instruments, much singing, and often liturgical dance as well.

Of course, radical differences separate the underlying worship theologies of Orthodox and charismatic traditions, but both focus on having an "encounter" with the living God, rather than merely learning about God. A full "baptism" of all the senses is seen as essential to foster this experience. This is the ethos of their traditions. The Presbyterian ethos also values the encounter with God. Within this ethos, however, that encounter is often sought more through the left-brained doors of rational discourse and retention of theological facts.

This discussion assumes that a clearly observable style of worship continues to be associated with a given denomination. But many observers report a breakdown in just such denominational worship distinctives.

Are Denominations
Losing Their Distinctiveness?

Fewer and fewer Christians are basing their decisions on which church to attend on denominational loyalty. Increasingly, even regular churchgoers are unclear about what makes their denomination different from another. For most, the differences they can identify have more to do with worship style than with theological issues. Decisions about what church to join are based on which church has the best children's and youth programs, music ministries, preaching style, or friendly atmosphere. In such a culture it is perhaps overoptimistic to assume that denominations have discernable personality traits. We may well be coming into an age when it is more

accurate to categorize congregations by worship style or theological views rather than merely by denomination. Yet, at least on the macro level, one can still identify a unique feel, ethos, or personality for various branches of the church at large.

Some traditions are noted for their use of visual imagery and symbolism, featuring artwork, incense, ceremony, and sacraments. Others are noted for services in which, after a few perfunctory preliminaries, a lengthy sermon designed to impart biblical and theological knowledge takes up most of the time. In others the lengthy sermon is evangelistic rather than pedagogical. Still other traditions prize the emotional encounter; if one hasn't *felt* God's presence during the worship time, one hasn't really worshiped.

It is easy to see that those who have been longtime members of a denomination or tradition feel a sense of loyalty to it and are influenced to no small degree by a sense of "fitting in" with that denominational personality. Those who have carefully and thoughtfully sought out and chosen to be a part of a given denominational tradition experience a similar fit. To their way of thinking, that tradition embodies a way of worship that seems most true to Scripture, or perhaps that just feels right to them. Some people seem naturally to lean toward traditions that value symbol and other nonverbal forms. Others will value the no-frills, no-nonsense practicality of a well-reasoned verbal exposition from the Bible. Both sides are likely to believe that their worship is pleasing to God. Depending on the strength of these proclivities and one's commitment to a particular biblical understanding of worship, each may believe that those who worship differently are the "weaker brother."

Among the many factors that will affect whether a congregation's ethos feels comfortable to a person is the way an individual's brain functions. A person with a strong left-brain preference will likely prefer the linear logic of a Presbyterian congregation, while someone with a strong right-brain preference will delight in the "smells and bells" of a Greek Orthodox service. Let's recall, however, that hemispheric differences in thinking are not simply a matter of right or left. A person's preferences may fall right in the middle between right and left, or anywhere in between. For a great many people, neither side of the brain is particularly dominant. The more nearly equal the influence of the two hemispheres, the

more the person is likely to adapt well to a variety of worship styles, even apart from the personality factors we have discussed. Thus, there seems to be good reason to suggest that cerebral hemispheric dominance may be a significant factor in determining denominational preference, and it may also help explain why many people feel no particular affinity to any one denominational ethos. Those who are fairly evenly balanced in the use of both cerebral hemispheres are better equipped to adjust to a wide variety of worship styles without feeling left out or inconvenienced.

So we see that hemispheric preferences can have direct linkages to denominational preferences. It is commonly believed that the growing number of denominations is one of the great failures of the Christian church. In many ways I agree. Our separations often speak of our lack of love, lust for power, and inability to discern the guiding of God's Holy Spirit. But insofar as the various denominations offer a variety of biblically justifiable worship styles, they provide a valuable service. While a great variety of worship styles may be found within most larger denominations, a single denomination will not offer the variety that currently exists across denominations—Southern Baptists, Episcopalians, Presbyterians, charismatic/Pentecostal, and independent churches, not to mention all the variety afforded by Third World churches and Western churches with a specific racial or ethnic connection. Nor do I see this sort of worship breadth developing in any one denomination in the foreseeable future. If the Reformation had never occurred, nor the earlier split between the Eastern and Western churches, and one holy Catholic Church still held forth, I suspect there would nonetheless be a need for radical differences in worship style from one congregation to another. People would still be looking for the congregation best suited to their needs. The monolithic worship style of medieval Catholic worship would not have survived intact in our modern world, at any rate. Sooner or later adaptations would have had to be made for the marvelous diversity of the people of God throughout the world.

Could it be that many of our differences in worship style are neither a disappointment nor a surprise to God? He may not be as partial to one worship style as we, in our myopia, may be tempted to assume. The God who created us with such diversity must surely

have known from the start that one worship style would never fit all—at least not in this life! Understanding the way God made our brains should prepare us to expect the same sort of diversity within our own denominations and even congregations.

We move now to explore some of the historical and theological factors that have served to form the personalities of mainstream Protestantism. The Lutheran and Reformed branches of the Reformation demonstrate two significantly different approaches to holistic brain issues. The theological constructs used to support these two positions are still in much use today. These differing streams of thought serve well to enlighten much about the current worship debates.

Calvin versus Luther

The current denominational divisions within Protestantism are a direct outgrowth of the great Reformation of the sixteenth century. The mainline denominations can still trace their lines of descent, with only a very few degrees of separation, directly back to Calvin and Luther. Presbyterian and Reformed denominations trace their lineage quite directly to Calvin's Geneva, with intervening side trips through Knox's Scotland, England's Westminster Assembly, or the Netherlands. Lutherans embrace their heritage by taking a direct flight back to Martin Luther's Germany. Anglicans and their American counterparts, the Episcopalians, had their own English Reformation, but the influence of Calvin and Geneva is etched deep in their Thirty-nine Articles and their continuing commitment to singing the Psalms. Methodism grows directly out of Anglicanism through John and Charles Wesley, who were both ordained ministers in the Church of England. American Baptists have their roots with Roger Williams, a dissenting Puritan from New England; and English Puritanism, in turn, has its roots in Calvinism.

While the distinctions among these denominations continue to deteriorate over time, as we have said, significant energy remains within each denomination, especially at higher governing and academic levels, to honor and maintain the ethos and heritage of the founders. In my associations with the leadership of various denomi-

nations over the years, I have observed a considerable fixation on the events of the sixteenth and seventeenth centuries as a foundation for these denominational identities. This is especially so in the Reformed constellation of denominations, in which adherence to the standards of the Westminster or Heidelberg Catechism can in some quarters become nearly as crucial to faithfulness as adherence to Scripture itself.[2] All too often, what gets forgotten in all the flag-waving is that roughly 15 centuries of Christian thought and experience preceded the lifetimes of their denominational founders.

One of the truly salutary benefits of the current liturgical renewal movement has been its success in reawakening us to the wisdom and insights of the early church. The effect for many has been similar to a sharp smack in the face, breaking our almost hypnotic obsession with the founders of our particular traditions and reconnecting us to the riches to be found in the collective wisdom of the church at large. This enlarged vision has done much to promote unity within the body of Christ. Of course, an obsession of any sort tends to restrict one's vision and to cloud one's thinking. Some have become so enamored of the early church and its ancient worship practices that the wisdom of the reformers has been overlooked. In either case, "There be dragons."

Since Luther and Calvin are the two major reformers, the primary streams from which Protestantism has flowed, let us now explore some of the factors that served to form the lasting ethos of each tradition. In so doing, we will see a number of quite distinctive features in each tradition and see as well how many of these features bear strong resemblance to characteristics commonly associated with either the right or left cerebral hemisphere. As was discussed in chapter 1, however, most neurologists are not even willing to concede that individuals truly exhibit a right- or left-brain dominance. If even this concept is thought to be too simplistic an assertion, I feel reasonably certain that the neurologists would never even consider that an entire religious denomination might exhibit right- or left-brain dispositions. What then gives me the audacity to proceed with this chapter? Quite simply, so many characteristics are commonly associated with each tradition—Lutheran and Calvinist—that correspond with well-established right- or left-

brain characteristics that it seems silly to pretend they are not there. Worshiping in a Lutheran church is a very different experience from worshiping in a Presbyterian or Reformed church. One could find more radical differences—say, Baptist versus Eastern Orthodox, but the very moderateness of both Lutherans and Presbyterians and their centrality within the European Reformation tradition make them a good pair for contrast. One need not find radical extremes to make the sorts of comparisons we propose to make. This point actually strengthens my argument.

So we will be talking unapologetically about right- and left-brain differences and boldly applying them to entire denominations, or at least to the basic historic ethos of each denomination. The differences speak for themselves and demonstrate how holistic engagement of the brain in worship is not as easy to come by as one may think. Further, it will demonstrate that people will often work very hard to excise elements of worship associated with one or the other sides of the brain.

The Lutheran Ethos

Martin Luther was not only a theologian but also a musician. He played the lute fairly well and clearly had a love and high regard for music. He composed the music for the great hymn "A Mighty Fortress" as well as others, wrote and arranged hymn texts, and gathered the best poets and musicians he could find to create a new body of congregational song for Germans to sing at worship. It is well known that Luther was not intent on leaving the Catholic Church but on reforming and purifying it. Luther valued, loved, and preserved much of the traditional Catholic musical, artistic, and liturgical treasury. He translated a number of the great old Latin hymns into German, reformatting their original tunes to match the new German translations. A prime example of this practice is the Easter hymn "Christ Lay in the Bonds of Death," which Luther arranged from the Latin hymn "Victimae Paschali Laudes."

Luther had obviously thought a great deal about the arts and their power to enrich life and enliven the mind. He believed that all the arts, as a great gift from God, could and must be enthusiasti-

cally encouraged and used by the church. The extent of his convictions in this regard is easy to discern in his writings:

> I am not of the opinion that all arts are to be cast down and destroyed on account of the Gospel, as some fanatics protest; on the other hand I would gladly see all arts, especially music, in the service of Him who has given and created them.[3]

Lutherans and Music

In typically colorful fashion, Luther expresses his enthusiasm for music in a foreword he wrote for a collection of choral motets by Georg Rhau:

> I would certainly like to praise music with all my heart as the excellent gift of God which it is and to commend it to everyone. . . . Next to the Word of God, music deserves the highest praise. . . . No greater commendation than this can be found—at least not by us. For whether you wish to comfort the sad, to terrify the happy, to encourage the despairing, to humble the proud, to calm the passionate, or to appease those full of hate . . . what more effective means than music could you find?
>
> Thus it was not without reason that the fathers and prophets wanted nothing else to be associated as closely with the Word of God as music. . . . After all, the gift of language combined with the gift of song was only given to man to let him know that he should praise God with both words and music, namely, by proclaiming the Word of God through music. . . .
>
> But when musical learning is added to all this and artistic music which corrects, develops, and refines the natural music, then at last it is possible to taste with wonder (yet not to comprehend) God's absolute and perfect wisdom in his wondrous work of music. Here it is most remarkable that one single voice continues to sing the melody, while at the same time many other voices play around it, exulting and adorning it in exuberant strains . . . so that those who are the least bit moved know nothing more amazing in this world. But any who remain unaffected are unmusical indeed and deserve to hear . . . the music of the pigs.[4]

Needless to say, under such leadership Lutherans have generated since their inception a prodigious stream of the finest religious music and art. The list of Lutheran composers of church music reads like a Who's Who of Western Culture's greatest musical masters: Heinrich Schütz, Johann Walther, Hans Leo Hassler, Johann Schein, Samuel Scheidt, Michael Praetorius, Dietrich Buxtehude, Georg Phillip Telemann, Johann Sebastian Bach (and his sons and his forbears), Georg Frideric Handel, Felix Mendelssohn, Johannes Brahms, and Hugo Distler.

These are the great ones. But more so than any other tradition, Lutheranism in America continues to provide a steady stream of church musicians who compose well for the average church choir and organist. The following is only a partial list: Jan Bender, Heinz Werner Zimmermann, Knut Nysted, Egil Hovland, David Johnson, Paul Manz, Robert Wetzler, S. Drummond Wolff, Carl Schalk, Donald Busarow, Richard Hillert, Philip Gehring, F. Melius Christiansen, Paul Christiansen, John Ferguson, Walter Pelz, Robert Hobby, Mark Sedio, Michael Burkhardt, and David Cherwien.

Lutheran colleges today are often noted for the excellence of their schools of music, and frequently the colleges and seminaries sponsor master's degree programs for the advanced training of church musicians. Especially in the Midwest, the singing tradition of the German and Scandinavian Lutherans is still alive and well. Church choirs there tend to be larger than in other parts of the country. St. Olaf College in Northfield, Minnesota, boasts one of the largest and most respected schools of music in the nation. A third of its entire student body is involved in some musical organization.[5] Luther College in Decorah, Iowa, has fully 40 percent of its student body involved in music.[6] Lutheran publishing houses such as Concordia, Augsburg Fortress, and Morningstar are among the most respected for the publication of high-quality church music.

Lutherans and Visual Imagery

As we shall see, Luther and Calvin differed on the use of visual imagery in worship. And that difference only grew more profound as the Lutheran and Reformed traditions developed on their separate tracks. Calvin saw virtually any pictorial representations—and especially images of the deity, even pictures of Christ while on

earth—as a grievous offense against the second of the Ten Commandments, "Thou shalt not make unto thee any graven image." Luther, in keeping with Roman Catholic practice, combines this injunction about graven images with the first commandment, "Thou shalt have no other gods before me." Ten commandments are retained by splitting the commandment on coveting into two separate commandments. In so doing, the issue of making "graven images" is de-emphasized by making it part of the First Commandment. He argues that it is not the images themselves that are at issue, but the worship of them.[7]

Though Luther spoke out vehemently against the use of images (painted or sculpted) that were contrary to God's Word, he had an increasing tolerance for them in general, seeing much value in retaining many forms of images. "That where there is a frequent preaching," he said, "there is no necessity of pictures; but will not every man add this, that if the true use of pictures be preached unto them, there is no danger of an abuse."[8] He added later, "There is nobody, or certainly very few, who do not understand that yonder crucifix is not my God, for my God is in heaven, but that is simply a sign."[9] John Calvin had less confidence that people could make that distinction.

While Calvinists removed virtually all forms of artwork from churches and even homes, Luther states:

> It is to be sure better to paint pictures on walls of how God created the world, how Noah built the ark, and whatever other good stories there may be, than to paint shamelessly worldly things. Yes, would to God that I could persuade the rich and mighty that they would permit the whole Bible to be painted on houses, on the outside and inside, so that all can see it. That would be a Christian work.[10]

In fact, Luther's German New Testament contained 21 woodcuts, including those famous Apocalypse pieces by Lucas Cranach. Later versions of Luther's Bible contained many more, with Luther himself deciding which biblical scenes should be depicted.[11] Some woodcuts depicting scenes of Lutheran worship feature a prominent crucifix right next to the pulpit, and one depicts Luther preaching while virtually brandishing a crucifix in one hand.[12]

Though first-generation Lutherans such as Andreas Carlstadt did their share of purging ecclesiastical art work that they believed was at odds with proper biblical belief, there was little of the wholesale iconoclasm so common in Calvinist circles. For his part, Luther was more concerned to educate people to the right use of visual images than simply to remove them wholesale. He had a basic trust that as God's Word began to be more fully understood by the laity, the Holy Spirit would slowly wean the people away from superstitious and vain uses of such things. "Abuses must be met as abuses, not as occasions for removing that which gives offense," he said. After all, anything could be used idolatrously.[13] Further, we know that Luther retained the basic design and adornments of his churches, except in instances where the pieces clearly referred to Catholic dogma rejected by the Reformation.

Many Lutheran churches I have visited have been exceptional in their creative and meaningful use of space and design, including a wide variety of symbolic features. It can be seen before one even enters the building in the traditional Lutheran red doors, signifying the blood of Christ through which we gain entrance into the Kingdom. When one enters the sanctuary, the eye is often drawn to some work of art rich in symbolic meaning. It may be a cross, a representation of Christ, a baptismal font, or a communion table. Rarely, in fact, is one's eye drawn to the pulpit as the focal point, as we will see is so often the case in a Reformed church. In the chancel area there may be a candle or other light inside red glass, constantly lit, signifying the eternal light of God. Many of these churches have a congregational seating design that promotes eye contact with fellow believers. In fact, emphasis on the *Gemeinde des Glaubens*, the gathered community of faith, is a major element in the Lutheran ethos. Once a worship service actually begins, we see many other ways symbolism and nonverbal communication abound.

Lutherans and Congregational Involvement

To be a part of a Lutheran worship service is to be kept constantly active. Congregational song continues to play a major role in the tradition. In addition to the inclusion of a number of hymns, Lutheran congregations traditionally sing large portions of their

liturgy. There is a musical dialogue between pastor and congregation surrounding the confession of sins and the readings of Holy Scripture and throughout the communion liturgy.

I attended a Lutheran service in Pennsylvania recently that employed the practice of reading the Gospel lesson in the midst of the congregation. After the Old Testament lesson, a psalm had been chanted responsively between a cantor and the congregation; then came a reading from an epistle. At the conclusion of the epistle reading, the organ immediately burst forth with the mighty sound of a majestic processional. Acolytes carrying lit candles and a very large Bible moved in procession from the chancel into the central aisle of the nave, with the minister following behind. When they arrived in the very center of the congregation, the music stopped, and the minister read the Gospel lesson from the Bible held by a lay assistant, while the two candle-bearers stood on either side, representing Christ, the Light of the World. As Jesus Christ is Emmanuel, "God with us," God himself come into our midst, so the writ-ten account of that incarnation was brought into the midst of the gathered congregation—symbol upon symbol. Following the Gospel reading, the congregation sang a brief thanksgiving for the Word. Then, once again, the organ pealed forth as the procession returned to the chancel area. Granted, this sort of high ceremony is not the norm in most Lutheran churches, but that it happens at all is indicative of an ethos that is at least occasionally open to such things.

Before that service began, I had an opportunity to discuss various aspects of church history with my 10-year-old nephew as, unprompted, he asked questions about who was depicted in the colorful stained-glass windows. Then he told me, "We need to check this place out after the service." His interest was not surprising to me, as he has already shown significant right-brained tendencies in his young life. Savoring this rare and precious opportunity for enlightened conversation with a 10-year-old, I was again reminded how shortsighted it is simply to attribute such liturgical acts to empty pomp and vainglory.

People with stronger right-brain dominance, especially in areas of music and visual symbolism, will likely feel a strong affinity with the Lutheran ethos, regardless of whether they can fully subscribe

to Lutheran theology. People with strong left-brained dominance may find this ethos to be saturated with empty formalities that have no positive effect on them at all. They may find themselves impatient with the liturgy as they wait, hoping the sermon will finally provide some real "meat" to chew on.

Indeed, the Lutheran tradition, for all its music and symbolism, also placed a high priority on the spoken word. At least into the eighteenth century, the typical three-hour Lutheran worship service devoted a full hour just to the sermon. But there was a rhythm and balance between right- and left-brained elements. The following outline of a typical Lutheran service in the mid-eighteenth century—a full two centuries after the time of Luther—demonstrates this balance. Note how saturated this service was with music. Even the prayers and Scripture lessons were sung, or at least chanted—a tradition stretching right back to the Old Testament synagogue. In fact, virtually the entire service was sung in one form or another.

Lutheran Epiphany Eucharist, Leipzig, Germany—1740[14]

Organ Prelude
Introit *(sung by choir)*
Organ Fantasia
Missa Brevis (Kyrie and Gloria) *(sung by choir)*
Collect *(chanted by pastor)*
Epistle *(chanted by pastor)*
Gradual Hymn
Gospel *(chanted by pastor)*
Toccata *(organ solo)*
Cantata *(choir and orchestra)*
Credal Hymn (Nicene Creed) *(sung by congregation)*
Pulpit Hymn *(sung by congregation)*
Sermon
Hymn *(sung by congregation)*
Organ Solo
Eucharistic Prayer *(partially chanted by pastor)*
Hymns during Communion *(sung by congregation)*
Post Communion Prayer *(chanted by pastor)*
Benediction

Final Hymn *(sung by congregation)*
Postlude

The Lutheran Ethos Today

But what of the Lutheran ethos today? How much of this right-brain emphasis is still evident in a typical Lutheran worship service in America? Robert Hawkins, professor of worship and music at Lutheran Theological Southern Seminary, Columbia, South Carolina, states that it depends on where you are. In the eastern United States, traditional worship with its rich use of the arts and frequent musical involvement of the entire congregation is still the norm. In the Midwest and far West, where church-growth patterns have taken a stronger hold, the current flood of musical and liturgical options has often obscured the traditional liturgical patterns. Replacing them is the newer praise-and-worship pattern of an extended period of song at the beginning of the service with less congregational participation thereafter than in a more traditional setting. Hawkins says that in the Midwest especially, the strong Scandinavian-Lutheran cultural ethos has always favored a simpler liturgy with less congregational involvement in the musical liturgy than in the East. These cultural factors have contributed to the growth of the praise-and-worship tradition in the Midwest.[15]

There is nothing in the more contemporary worship styles that seems necessarily to indicate a shift in right-left brain emphasis for Lutherans. If Hawkins is accurate in his geographical appraisal of Lutheran worship practices, places that made less use of liturgical music and other art forms in the past will continue to do so today, though the styles of music and the format of the liturgy has changed. In other locales, the East in particular, Lutherans have generally not lost their richer musical and artistic life. There are roughly 9.5 million Lutherans of various denominations in the United States.[16] Most Lutherans immigrated to America in the eighteenth and nineteenth centuries. Most of today's Lutherans are generations away from their immigrant forebears. Yet ethnic and cultural characteristics can run deep. We should only expect to see significant variations in the worship life of so many people and not expect to see cultural trends uniformly apparent throughout all of Lutheranism.

The Reformed Ethos

The other major stream flowing from the great Reformation is the Reformed tradition, springing from Ulrich Zwingli and John Calvin. From this fountainhead come the Puritans, Presbyterians, and other denominations using the word "Reformed" in their names. These denominations have their major geographical roots in Switzerland, France, England, Scotland, and the Netherlands.

It will be instructive right from the start to compare a typical example of a Reformed worship service with the Lutheran service outlined above:

John Knox's *Form Of Prayers*—1556[17]

Confession of Sin
Psalm *(sung in unaccompanied unison by congregation)*
Scripture and Sermon
Prayer for the Whole Christian Church
Lord's Prayer
Creed *(sometimes sung by congregation)*
Psalm *(sung by congregation)*
Blessing/Benediction *(end of typical service)*
* * *
Lord's Supper *(celebrated roughly four times a year)*
Words of Institution
Exhortation *(self-examination and fencing of the table)*
Thanks for the Bread *(seated at a table)*
Distribution *(Scripture read)*
Prayer of Thanksgiving
Psalm 103 *(sung by congregation)*

The Reformed movement got its first major thrust through the work of the Swiss reformer Ulrich Zwingli. Zwingli was even more musical than Luther, having studied music as part of his rigorous education in the humanities. But though he loved and even composed music, still he oversaw by 1527 the dismantling of all organs in Zurich and the whitewashing of church walls. To his way of

thinking, nothing appealing to the senses should be allowed to distract worshipers from hearing the Word of God, and by that he meant the reading of Scripture and its explication in the sermon—this and nothing more. In fact, Zwingli banned all music from his Reformed services of worship. Not only instruments but any form of singing was disallowed.[18] This seems strange, indeed, coming from a man who could play 11 musical instruments. Elements in Zwingli's developing theology, based always on an unwavering biblicism as he understood it, however, seemed to overrule his musical affinities when it came to matters of worship.[19]

It was not only music making that was disallowed. In Zurich and its environs, the arts virtually died out altogether for a time. In other places where this branch of the Reformation held forth, artists continued to work but soon learned to limit themselves to landscapes, portraits, still lifes, or historical subjects, as opposed to any religious subjects.[20]

It is with Zwingli that we see the formation of what was later to be known as the Regulative Principle. In its classical form, as developed by the Puritans, this principle states, "[W]ith regard to worship whatever is commanded in Scripture is required, and that whatever is not commanded is forbidden."[21] This line of thought is seen already in Zwingli, however. He becomes convinced that Holy Scripture—not church or tradition—would be his only source for spiritual truth. If a worship activity was not explicitly called for in the Bible, it had no business being practiced within the church.[22]

Yet, there is something in Zwingli's thinking that runs counter to Scripture and even smacks of dualism.[23] James F. White, professor of liturgical studies at Drew University, addresses this issue in his book *Protestant Worship*:

> Zwingli's teaching and practices were introducing a strain that might seem at odds with the biblical revelation: a disregarding of the physical world as a means of conveying the spiritual. Zwingli believed that "it is clear and indisputable that no external element or action can purify the soul," and thus it was completely consistent to discount the use of physical objects and actions in worship. A sense of the sign value[24] of things in conveying God's grace is altogether lacking. This disjuncture between the physical and

spiritual sets Zwingli apart from Luther and Calvin. Essentially it
is a matter of piety. If the physical cannot lead one to God, one
has drawn a circle around much of the traditional Christian cultus
and marked it for destruction.[25]

There are times in Christian history when theologies arise that
suggest that the material world is less godly than the spiritual world;
some have even gone so far as to say that the physical world is evil.
White points out that Zwingli's theology of worship bears certain
similarities to such thinking. A more biblical perspective celebrates
all of creation as God's handiwork, proclaimed by the Creator to
be "very good."

In fairness, it must be clearly stated that for Zwingli, as for
Calvin in the next generation, these limitations on worship do not
spring from the anti-aesthetic ravings of an unsophisticated boor,
as many claim. In his commentary on Genesis 4:20-21, Calvin makes
this clear: "For the invention of arts . . . is a gift of God by no
means to be despised, and a faculty worthy of commendation."[26]
The limitations on worship are, rather, brought on by men who
loved and honored the arts and artists. Their commitment to the
absolute preeminence of Scripture, however, led them to enact liturgical policies that went no further than what the Bible expressly
stated.

While John Calvin, chief Reformed figure of the next generation, did not go as far as Zwingli in these matters, the restrictions
against most (not all) right-brained elements in worship were further institutionalized under his guidance. The following extended
quotation from his *Institutes of the Christian Religion* states his
position plainly enough:

> As a child (says Paul) is guided by his tutor according to the ca-
> pacity of his age, so the Jews were under the custody of the law
> (Gal. 4:1-3). But we are like adults, who, freed of tutelage and
> custody, have no need of childish rudiments. . . . Therefore, if we
> wish to benefit the untutored, raising up a Judaism that has been
> abrogated by Christ is a stupid way to do it. . . . Under Moses the
> spiritual worship [John. 4:23] of God was figured and, so to speak,

enwrapped in many ceremonies; but now that these are abolished, he is worshiped more simply. Accordingly, he who confuses this difference is overturning an order instituted and sanctioned by Christ.

Shall no ceremonies then (you will ask) be given to the ignorant to help them in their inexperience? I do not say that. For I feel that this kind of help is very useful to them. I only contend that the means used ought to show Christ, not to hide him. Therefore God has given us a few ceremonies, not at all irksome, to show Christ present. To the Jews more were given as images of Christ were absent. He was absent, I say, not in power, but in the means by which he might be made known. Accordingly, to keep that means, it is necessary to keep fewness in number, ease in observance, dignity in representation, which also includes clarity.[27]

Consequently, . . . I approve only those human constitutions which are founded upon God's authority, drawn from Scripture, and, therefore, wholly divine. . . . The Lord has in his sacred oracles faithfully embraced and clearly expressed both the whole sum of true righteousness, and all aspects of the worship of his majesty, and whatever was necessary to salvation; therefore, in these the Master alone is to be heard. But because he did not will in outward discipline and ceremonies to prescribe in detail what we ought to do (because he foresaw that this depended upon the state of the times, and he did not deem one form suitable for all ages), here we must take refuge in those general rules which he has given, that whatever the necessity of the church will require for order and decorum should be tested against these. Lastly, because he has taught nothing specifically, and because these things are not necessary to salvation, and for the upbuilding of the church ought to be variously accommodated to the customs of each nation and age, it will be fitting (as the advantage of the church will require) to change and abrogate traditional practices and to establish new ones. Indeed, I admit that we ought not to charge into innovation rashly, suddenly, for insufficient cause. But love will best judge what may hurt or edify; and if we let love be our guide, all will be safe.[28]

Needless to say, these passages deserve careful unpacking and interpretation on many levels. One key issue here is Calvin's understanding of the relationship between the Old Testament and the New. In his commentary on Psalm 92:4 we read:

> In the fourth verse, he more immediately addresses the Levites, who were appointed to the office of singers, and calls upon them to employ their instruments of music—not as if this were in itself necessary, only it was useful *as an elementary aid* to the people of God in these ancient times. We are not to conceive that God enjoined the harp as feeling a delight like ourselves in mere melody of sounds; but the Jews, *who were yet under age*, were astricted [limited] to the use of *such childish elements* [italics added].[29]

The idea is that with the coming of the fuller revelation of God and his will that we have in Jesus Christ, God has established a New Covenant or Testament, a more excellent covenant that paves the way for a more mature form of worship—that propounded in the New Testament. We note the connection Calvin makes between musical instruments, ceremonies, and childishness. We in the New Testament church have the full maturity of God's Revelation. The Old Testament Jews did not, and functioned under "childish rudiments."

Now insofar as this charge of immaturity refers to the sacrificial system and its associated ceremonies, we must heartily, fully, and thankfully agree with Calvin. We in the New Covenant have in Christ the one full and final sacrifice for sin. The death and resurrection of Jesus Christ marked the end of the entire Old Testament sacrificial system, along with all its ceremonies and accoutrements. But there is a distinction here that many Reformed theologians seem to overlook. Even Calvin seems to assume that the abolition of the sacrificial system means that there is no longer any need for all the symbolic nonverbal elements in worship we explored in chapter 3—no need for vestments, color, candlesticks, incense, musical instruments, skillfully made furnishings or art. No need, for that matter, for preaching styles rich in pictorial illustrations or other elements that arouse the right-brained imagination.

The actual value of symbolism or nonverbal communication is only rarely discussed by Calvin. The closest he gets is to hurl invectives against vain ceremonies, as in the excerpt above. But these diatribes are always connected to his opposition to the lavish ceremony of the Roman eucharistic celebrations. In fact, it is the medieval Roman theology and complexity of the mass he is really attacking, not the concept of ceremony or symbolism per se. In fact, when he writes about the proper celebration of the sacraments, his approach to ceremony and symbolism is more positive, though even there he issues warnings that simplicity is the order of the day. The second section of the preceding excerpt from Calvin's *Institutes* is a typical example.

So while it is true that the sacrificial death of Christ eliminated the need for the Old Testament sacrificial system, this does not mean that God is no longer concerned about communicating by means of the symbolic and other nonverbal forms of communication associated with the Old Testament temple, as Calvin suggests. God's concern about right-brained ways of communicating and knowing are based not in the sacrificial system, not in the Tabernacle or Temple cults in general, not even in the nature of the Old Covenant versus the New. God's interest in addressing the whole brain is deeply rooted in the Creator's affirmation that material objects are "good"—"very good," in the inherent nonverbal communicative power of the entire created order, in the implications of the *Imago Dei*, and in God's gracious insistence upon visible signs—his gifts given to confirm his promises. God's concern for holistic communication is further emphasized in the imaginative parables of Jesus, in the inclusion of poetry and apocalyptic in Scripture, and not least in water, wine, and bread.

The practical ramifications of this Reformed perspective on worship is that though Calvin did allow congregational singing, it was limited to unaccompanied unison singing of the Psalms and a few other texts, such as the Ten Commandments, the Nunc Dimitis,[30] and the Creed. The dismantling or destruction of pipe organs continued throughout the churches where Calvinism held sway. The great organ in the cathedral in Geneva was silenced. Not until the nineteenth century were the strains of a pipe organ to be heard

there again. Statues and other pieces of art were destroyed, or at least removed from churches. All adult choirs were disbanded. Sometimes these were replaced by children's choirs, but the children's choral repertoire was strictly limited to learning the new metrical settings of the Psalms in order to teach them to the adults. Nothing was to be retained that would encourage a return to the errors and superstitions of the Roman Church or that might distract people from paying attention to the words of the minister.

It was in these ways that the cult of words—and, frankly, words directed to the left brain—was begun and deeply established in the Reformed ethos. Barbara Kiefer Lewalski, Harvard professor of English literature, in discussing five different British Protestant preaching styles as documented by a seventeenth century observer, describes the Presbyterian style as follows:

> The sermon in the manner of the Presbyterians displays their highly complex scholastic divisions and subdivisions of the text into doctrines, reasons, and uses, with numerous points and subclassifications under each head; their logical, undecorated style; and their habit of persistent Scripture quotations.[31]

It is not my purpose to pass a harsh judgment on this tradition. It is, after all, my own adopted tradition. If the opinions and actions of the Reformed Christians seem severe to us today, we must remember the ecclesiastical situations that spurred such edicts, as well as prompting many of the reforms sought by Luther. Just imagine what Herculean efforts it surely took to break the spell that medieval Roman Catholicism had cast upon the average person! Consider the Roman Church's utter fascination with all things connected to the saints—their feast days, romantic legends, relics, and the prayers to saints. Recall the state of the Eucharist—the use of Latin, which no layperson understood, the theology of transubstantiation, the rampant superstitions, the fear of desecrating the very body of Christ, and thus the infrequency with which the average person communed. We must remember the eye-crossing complexity of the ceremonies that had accumulated around the mass over the centuries. Virtually all music within the mass was performed by professionals—and in Latin, not by the congregation

and not in the people's own language. When nearly every statue or painting was believed to be an infringement of the Second Commandment or a temptation to return to Roman tradition or theology, we too might have found ourselves joining cries to tear them down. If every organ was a reminder that the active worship of the laity had been totally usurped by the clergy and professional orders, one might be tempted even today to destroy all the organs. At a time when the written and preached Word of God had been kept from the people for so long and was finally restored through the reformers, we, too, might have wished to eliminate aspects of corporate worship that might distract people from being instructed in the verbal proclamation of that Word. The need for clear, pure teaching was indeed dire.

Thus was firmly established the particularly lean traditions of English and Scottish Reformed worship in the founding of America and of America's psyche about worship. The cult of simplicity was further strengthened as Americans came to associate any sort of pomp and ceremony with England and England's king. The American Revolution pretty well decided what this nation thought about such things.

I once had lunch with an elderly layman who had been a lifelong southern Presbyterian. We were discussing matters related to Christian worship. Toward the end of the discussion, he sat back in his chair and with an air of quiet certitude, stated, "The simpler the better." That served as his summary of proper Reformed worship. The less ceremony, the less complication, the less musical embellishment, the less symbolism, the better. And that is not a bad summary of much of the historical Reformed approach to worship. It is an ethos that has great appeal to the "no-nonsense" mind-set, or to those who prefer or are at least content with the left-brained world of words and orderly verse-by-verse expository preaching.

Reformed Architecture

Finally, a brief examination of Reformed church architecture and design is in order. As with the Lutherans, early Calvinists tended to make use of the church buildings currently available, that is to say, Catholic buildings. Unlike the Lutherans, Calvinists made fairly

radical changes to these church interiors. In medieval Catholic worship, people were unable to hear the ornately robed priests as they murmured their Latin liturgies in a far removed chancel area. They were expected to stand in the nave in silent meditation or to wander around the room using the biblical scenes and characters portrayed in windows, statues, or paintings to rehearse in their minds the various biblical accounts.

After the sixteenth century Reformation, the congregation had a more central role—to listen to the sermon preached by a minister in decidedly nonliturgical garb. So in addition to the iconoclasm, interior designs were readapted to meet Reformed worship needs. The chancel area was generally abandoned, and a simple pulpit and table were placed in the nave area or center of the church or cathedral. As the focus of worship changed from spatial and visual to verbal and aural, there was suddenly a need to gather around a pulpit to hear a lengthy sermon. Reformed church design favored some sort of wrap-around plan. Benches were installed, usually in concentric circles around the pulpit. Catholic critics were quick to observe that Calvinist churches tended to look and function more like schools than places of worship.[32]

As opportunity arose to build new worship spaces, Reformed congregations tended toward an architectural plan designed specifically for such Reformed worship. The "meetinghouse" was born. As might be expected, these were often circular in construction, so that the congregation could easily gather around the Word and Table. Even when a basic rectangular shape was retained, the central focus was on the pulpit, and secondarily on the table. As Reformed architecture was institutionalized over the ensuing years, this format became fairly standard. The meetinghouse was a single room with the pulpit in the center of one wall. Benches were installed either in a circle or later in pew boxes arranged in various sections, but all oriented toward the pulpit.

Of course, architectural ornamentation was kept to a bare minimum. Nothing was to detract attention from the pulpit. But this plainness should not be equated with ugliness or lack of creative skill. Reformed worship spaces may be relatively simple affairs, but there is generally much beauty. Builders put their creative skills to work in graceful staircases, elegant moldings, and other beauti-

fully finished wood and metal work. Such rooms, with their clean white walls and ceilings, can impart a wonderful sense of proportion and peace. The currently popular New England Shaker style of architecture and furniture may not be strictly "Reformed," but it certainly gives us a well-recognized example of American Puritan influence. It is indeed beautiful and in its own way speaks of the values and beliefs of those who designed and built it.

The Reformed Ethos Today

Much has changed in twentieth and twenty-first century Reformed circles, and an increasing number of voices are calling for a reexamination of the historic Reformed worship ethos and its biblical underpinnings.[33] Hymns and pipe organs became ever more common as the nineteenth century unfolded. Reformed congregations today are as likely as any to hire a full-time church musician and to develop a full-orbed music program complete with handbells, brass quartet, praise band, and annual concert series. Calvin's Geneva gown, once worn as a rejection of clerical garb, has now itself become a clerical garment. Reformed architecture, though still comparatively reserved, has generally lost its ethos of radical simplicity. Images are rarely seen as idolatrous, and vibrant color from choir and clergy robes, stained glass, and banners fills Reformed sanctuaries. In instances where such Reformed churches have not lost their strong tradition of solid biblical preaching and theological integrity based on their historic creeds and confessions, this tradition is perhaps better poised than ever to minister to the whole human mind.

Currently the Reformed family exhibits at least as much diversity about worship as the Lutheran family. Two trends are having a significant impact on this ethos, however—the liturgical renewal movement and the various forms of contemporary worship. As with many other church bodies, Presbyterian and Reformed denominations have adopted to a significant degree the agenda of the broader liturgical reform movement which, as stated earlier, calls for a return to worship practices from the early church, rather than a fixation on the period of reformers and founders. Major emphases in this movement are a push for weekly celebrations of the

Lord's Supper and increased attention to the seasons of the church calendar. Much of this agenda adds significant right-brained emphasis. This is certainly true of the sacraments, as has been discussed. An increased focus on the church year might manifest itself in the use of paraments[34] displaying the seasonal colors, banners, advent wreaths, or such special services as Tenebrae, foot-washing, or healing services, including anointing with oil. Virtually all of this agenda heads in a new direction from the classical Reformed ethos.

Second, as elsewhere, contemporary worship trends have made significant inroads into almost every denomination in the Reformed family. Whether one calls it "contemporary worship," "praise and worship," or "seeker-sensitive worship," the elements are about the same. One generally finds a rather lengthy segment of singing replacing the traditional call to worship and opening hymn. Regardless of the musical style, the effect is to reverse radically the ratio of music to spoken word in favor of music, at least in the beginning of the service. This movement is also known for including brief dramas as part of the worship service, frequently just before the sermon. These dramas tend to set the stage for the sermon by focusing attention on a particular issue or exemplifying the sort of problem the sermon might address. Interestingly, such modern dramas seek to achieve about the same thing early Lutherans sought to achieve by placing a lengthy choral cantata based upon the Gospel reading just before the sermon. Both serve to set the stage for a more perceptive hearing of the sermon, and both seek to achieve this through more right-brained avenues.

Drama, music, frequent sacraments, banners, colors, symbols, and symbolic services—all these introduce strong stimulation for the right brain, and all are relatively new to the Presbyterian/Reformed tradition. They remain divisive in many circles. The degree to which such elements become common will indicate the degree to which the Presbyterian/Reformed ethos evolves into a new thing.

Yet, though signs of change are evident in the Presbyterian and Reformed ethos, there is still much to suggest that the ethos is intact. Using music again as an example, one notes that the spiritual heirs of Calvin have produced virtually no great composers other

than Jan Sweelinck, and he is hardly a household name even among musicians! We are hard pressed as well to produce a list of prominent contemporary Reformed church music composers. One might include such names as John Weaver and K. Lee Scott, but the stark contrast with the Lutheran tradition speaks for itself. Further, there are no nationally recognized schools of music associated with any of the lengthy list of Presbyterian and Reformed colleges and universities, many of which enjoy magnificent academic reputations. None of them has developed equal prominence in music—or in any area of the arts, for that matter. Further, at this writing, the only master's degree program in church music offered by a Reformed educational institution is the program I developed at Erskine College and Seminary. This is not to say that there are no excellent fine arts programs in Presbyterian and Reformed colleges. I know of two fine Presbyterian collegiate music programs in my immediate geographical area. I teach at one of them! But these are hardly of national prominence.

Summary

Thus we see how a particular personality or ethos can be associated with a denominational or theological tradition. We further see that a denomination may have a natural tendency toward right- or left-brainedness. Especially in such traditions, special care should be taken to make sure that worship will regularly provide food for the whole brain. Otherwise, for some, worship will remain an often exhausting process; it is hard work to maintain attention and interest in a service constantly directed to one's less agile cerebral hemisphere.

Our examination of the ethos of various worship traditions reminds us that history is a living thing. The decisions of those who have gone before us have a way of resonating far into the future. In the next chapter we will explore other ways the past lives on today and affects, sometimes profoundly, the ways we worship. We will continue to see as well how issues of cerebral hemispheric preference are in evidence all along the way.

Questions for Thought and Discussion

1. Discuss the ethos of worship from your current church home, and compare this with other experiences of worship familiar to you.
2. Based on what you learned from this chapter, what worship forms speak most clearly to your heart, mind, and soul?
3. What aspects of denominational personalities would you include in corporate worship? What aspects would you eliminate?
4. From your answers to these questions, are your preferences based in primarily right- or left-brain function or in a balance between the two?

Chapter Seven

Reflections from an English Cathedral

All beauty speaks of Thee: the mountains and the rivers,
the line of lifted sea where spreading moonlight quivers.
The deep-toned organ blast that rolls through arches dim,
hints of the music vast of Thine eternal hymn.
                                    —*Edward Grubb, 1925*

I recently had the privilege of spending two weeks in England, the first week in Salisbury and the next in Cambridge. One of my goals for this trip was to immerse myself in the worship life of a great and historic cathedral. Salisbury Cathedral most certainly qualified, as it has been a center for Christian worship since 1225. Accordingly, over a period of six days I attended 14 worship events: four early-morning Eucharists, six evensongs, an evening healing service with Eucharist, an afternoon Eucharist following the 1662 order of service, a service celebrating the Cathedral's special relationship with the Anglican Diocese of the Sudan, and a Sunday-morning high Eucharist. Then, while in Cambridge, I attended an additional 10 evensong services: six at King's College Chapel, three at St. John's College Chapel, and one at Clare College Chapel.

Although work on this book was already in progress when I took this trip, I had no specific agenda for those weeks beyond what I stated above. But as I returned home and continued my research and writing, I found myself reminded over and over of experiences I had in Salisbury and Cambridge. I saw many examples of how architecture and symbolism had communicated with me, engaging my right brain on a multitude of levels. I felt in new and instructive ways the impact of those gathered with me for worship. I learned that history is still with us today. The results of the

actions taken by medieval builders and by leaders of the sixteenth century English Reformation are still there to be seen—still physically having their effect on today's worship. I was therefore reminded that the worship revisions we engage in today may also have a rippling effect well beyond our own years, for we too are in a time of profound change in worship. In England I was steeped in history but engaged in real worship with real people in modern times. One reason that this book deals so much with worship history is that we are all living with the ramifications of what has been done in the past. History not only helps us understand why we worship as we do today; it is a real entity right there in the pews with us—part of the communion of the saints, if you will. Here is some of what I learned.

What the Cathedral Said

Like so many American Protestants, I have been strongly influenced in my worship and devotional experience by frontier revivalism and pietism in general. While I am no stranger to higher liturgical settings, I hoped that in an English cathedral I would have access to a worship life that was much more strongly linked to ancient worship forms. And, at any rate, it would be different simply because I was in England, not America—the old world, not the new.

When one studies the factors that led the medieval world to build such grand structures, one recurrent theme is that the massiveness and extreme height of these edifices were intended to make one feel small and insignificant in comparison to the greatness of God (and the church). In short, they were a "power statement." The stunning beauty of such structures witnessed to the beauty and perfections of the Creator, starkly contrasting with the obvious imperfections and ugly sinfulness of the worshiper. It is all but impossible for a person of the twenty-first century to imagine the impact such a structure would have had on a medieval peasant. And even today, though many buildings are taller and larger than cathedrals, one rarely enters a structure whose *interior* is more cavernous than that of a medieval cathedral. The effect is still striking, if not overwhelming.

In addition to the many services I attended at Salisbury Cathedral, I took ample time simply to sit and be still. I came to worship services early and often stayed until the kindly verger informed me that it was time for him to lock the doors. I took much free time, not just to tour the many facets of this amazing building but to sit quietly in different parts of the building and meditate. Yet in all this time, I did not get the sense of feeling overwhelmed by the sheer scope of the structure. Perhaps this is because I have become rather well traveled over the years and have been in many such structures. Perhaps it is that my theological training too thoroughly drummed into my head that I, even I, am a focal point of God's immense grace and love. If I was dwarfed by this cathedral, God's covenant, established with me personally, dwarfs the cathedral.

So the cathedral did not make me feel insignificant, intimidated, or particularly sinful. I viewed it from the security of my position as a forgiven child of God. Yet the building was clearly speaking to me. It simply felt good to be there. It was easy to spend long periods of time sitting quietly, often not thinking about much of anything. As I considered later what was happening to me in the cathedral, I realized that the place imparted to me feelings of vastness, grandeur, and *great* peace. The peacefulness seemed to come from the building's beauty, quietness, and symmetry.

Everywhere I looked I saw the beauty of excellence. Every object was in its own way a work of art and worthy of special consideration. Everywhere I went, the cathedral was speaking words of peace to me. Cathedrals are generally quiet places—generally, but not always. The more famous the cathedral, the more tourists, and with the tourists comes an immense amount of noise. A house of worship is transformed into at best a museum, at worst a cacophonous bazaar. I have been in St. Paul's Cathedral in London at times when I could relate to literally nothing of the original purpose of the building. The massive space was swarming—better, writhing—with a restless sea of sightseers. Numerous booths were set up to sell religious kitsch, CDs of the choir and organ, and other tourist treasures, and the vast acoustic was a din of chatter, footsteps, and cash registers. I prayed for Jesus to come at once and cleanse his temple! Perhaps he did. The last time I was there, the cathedral was charging a significant admission fee, and as a result, only those

truly interested were inside. And there was only one modest sales booth, located right next to the admission gate. This time a person could better engage in quiet prayer or simply get a sense of the holy. Salisbury in November has no such tourist interest, and the quietness could be quite profound, especially early in the morning.

The sense of peacefulness came to me, in part, as a result of Salisbury's architectural symmetry. The overall length of the cathedral interior is a staggering 449 feet—or as long as one and a half U.S. football fields. Upon entering the space, one sees two long rows of thick blackish marble pillars dividing the central nave (the main part of a worship room, the congregational space) from the side aisles. On each side, the tall pillars support graceful Gothic (pointed) arches. When one looks down the central nave of such a cathedral, one has a unique experience of architectural symmetry and perspective. The matching pillars and arches on each side seem to get lower and closer together as one's eyes follow them forward. As I absorbed this sight over and over throughout the week, it never failed to instill a sense of calm. Especially when one sat in the midst of the pillars and arches, they were like undulating waves, gently rocking, rocking, rocking. For me, it was at times almost as if God himself were rocking me.

Salisbury Cathedral, looking east from the central western doors.[1]

Salisbury Cathedral from the western triforium, showing the relationship of the triforium arches to the ground-floor arches.[2]

Soon the observer's eyes ascend to see that these pillars and arches support yet another arcade of pillars and arches, also proceeding the full length of the nave. This higher arcade, known as the triforium, is of smaller scale, but the arches are more ornate and rounded. The undulating rhythm of this arcade plays in counterpoint with that of the lower. While there is much here to analyze mathematically and geometrically as well as artistically, viewing such an arcade of columns and arches is a remarkable experience whether one analyzes it or not.

Much could also be said of the windows, the various chapels, and the superlative music from the choirs and organ. But the architectural features cited above are merely a few examples of how the stones of the building themselves communicated through their beauty, quiet, and symmetry what I have come to believe was God's own peace.

Interestingly, the room did not make me feel particularly "religious." It did not inspire in me any specifically theological or spiri-

tual thoughts—at least, not right away. But being in a medieval cathedral is a unique experience, and as such the place imparted its own special mystique. Part of that mystique, for me, came from an awareness that from this very place have ascended untold prayers, countless holy acts and expressions of faith, and the unbroken proclamation of Word and Sacrament for well over 700 years. This realization was not mere sentimentality; I was well aware that this place was also the scene of countless sins of pride, vanity, ecclesiastical and political machination and corruption, and heresies of every sort. But these sorry facts no more spoiled this place than those same crimes erase the true glory of the universal church. I leave it to the Lord to separate the wheat from the chaff. I gloried in the harvest of wheat I knew must surely have been sown there.

As the days went by, my sense of awe abated. I found myself confidently walking from one location to another with much less thought about the splendor all around me. All too soon I started to take the place for granted, to accept it as the norm. While this was a bit disappointing to me and more than a little instructive, I also observed that the initial impact of awe was being replaced by a growing sense of comfort and still more peace. When I chose to lay aside my personal cares and concerns, my constant sense that I had better move on if I wanted to see all the sights of Salisbury, and allowed myself to simply "be" in that space, it still spoke warmly to my soul, even in an English November! I could feel my breathing slow down, and the tension in my shoulders slowly relax. And then the gentle rocking of the pillars and arches, the glory of the stained glass, the quietness, the very vastness of the place again addressed their unspoken words to my soul. I began to sense how it could take a lifetime for this special place to say all that it might to one who had ears and eyes to hear and see.

The War against Color

I chose Salisbury Cathedral for my visit in part because of Edward Rutherfurd's epic novel *Sarum*,[3] which I had read a number of times. This work of historical fiction traces the history of Salisbury and the surrounding Wiltshire countryside from prehistory through

modernity. Sarum was the ancient name for Salisbury, an important Christian center from very early times. In fact, in old Sarum, two miles away, St. Osmund built a sizable cathedral that was consecrated in 1092, two centuries before the present cathedral was completed. In one chapter, Rutherfurd chronicles the events surrounding the construction of the present thirteenth century cathedral. He describes the day one of the leading cathedral masons brought his son to see it for the first time:

> If the outside of the building was impressive, the inside was astonishing. It was not only the huge, spacious nave and side aisles which seemed, like huge tunnels, to disappear into the distance, not only the airy transepts, flooding the center of the church with light: it was the fact that the whole of the inside was painted. For the Gothic cathedral of the medieval world was a riot of color. The vaults, the pillars, the carvings and the tombs that lay in the chantry chapels were all painted in brilliant blues, reds, and greens. The effect was as bright and vivid as the marketplace; its carved and painted foliage seemed as lush as the Avon valley from which they had come. As the little boy gazed enraptured down the lines of graceful pillars he cried: "It's like a forest." And so it was. [4]

This section of Rutherfurd's book always intrigued me, since I had been to many English cathedrals, and few if any I had seen could be described as "a riot of color." Stained-glass windows and perhaps a few banners were the main relief offered to the uniform tans and grays of the stonework. It was during a guided tour of the cathedral tower that I finally came to understand how and when the change occurred. Once again, I learned it was the edicts of the sixteenth century reformers that had ordered the removal of all the painting from Salisbury cathedral, and from most other cathedrals as well. Many of the leaders of the English Reformation had escaped to Calvin's Geneva during the Catholic reign of Queen Mary I (also known as "Bloody Mary" or Mary Tudor).There they absorbed much (but not all) of the Reformed perspective on liturgical matters, bringing it back to England when Elizabeth I revived the Church of England once and for all. So, as in other areas where Calvinism rather than Lutheranism flourished, churches were

stripped not only of relics, statues, musical instruments, and other offending artwork, but of as much color as might be reasonably removed. Entire walls and ceilings were whitewashed, apparently even when they featured only abstract designs or solid colors.

"If you want to see what Salisbury Cathedral probably looked like," our guide told us, "go downtown to St. Thomas' Church and observe their Doom Painting on the chancel arch above the pulpit and lectern." He informed us that this painting, too, was white-washed over by the Reformers but was later restored through a painstaking process. I took his advice and found my way the next day to St. Thomas' Church.

Fifteenth-century St. Thomas' Church is the Anglican parish church for Salisbury, located right by an ancient center-city marketplace. The Doom Painting is huge and impossible to miss as one enters the building. As I studied the painting, I marveled that it was marked for destruction by the Reformers. What was it about the painting that they objected to? As can be seen on the next page, Christ is seated on his throne of judgment. All seems to be as depicted in Matthew 25 in the parable of the sheep and the goats. People are arising from their graves at the sound of the last trumpet. Those on Christ's right are admitted into the New Jerusalem. Those on Christ's left are raised up, only to be herded by a demon into the mouth of hell, which is depicted as the mouth of a great dragon.

Careful examination reveals that a king and a queen are among those headed for hell. Interestingly, there is a damned bishop right behind them. But there is also a bishop being raised to eternal life on Christ's right.

Study this picture as I might, I could find nothing in it that contradicts the plain teaching of Scripture. Actually, since one of the bishops is portrayed as going to hell, I see more reason for Catholics to be offended than Protestants. So what led the Protestant reformers to take such drastic action here? In this instance, it was probably the fact that the painting portrays Christ on his judgment throne, and the English reformers were largely convinced that any visual portrayal of the Father, Son, or Holy Spirit was a breaking of the Second Commandment. What is more, Protestant art of the Reformation period tends to avoid depicting the Last Judgment, as it had a strong association with the Catholic dogmas of salvation by works rather than by grace through faith.[7] But I suspect

The doom painting on the chancel arch of St. Thomas' Church, Salisbury, England, depicting the last judgment of Christ.[5]

The lower right portion of the doom painting, depicting the condemned souls being herded into the mouth of a dragon.[6]

that the objections ran deeper than these dogmas. As with the painted walls in the cathedral, reformers felt obliged to remove anything that might distract the worshiper from giving full concentration to the words spoken by the minister. And it was in that regard an attack, however well-intentioned, against our God-given right brains.

War against Images

Much has been written documenting this wide-scale purging of visual images and how it spread beyond the church into society in general and even into private homes. Ernest Gilman, professor of English at New York University, offers a typical example:

> The Royal Visitors' Injunctions, published in July 1547, warned the clergy against "the most detestable offence of idolatry" and directed incumbents to remove and "utterly extinct and destroy" all paintings and other monuments of superstition, not only on the walls or in the windows of churches, but in private houses as well. By 1550, as Laurence Stone notes, "whole shiploads of religious statuary were being exported to France. . . ."[8]
> In 1560 the accounts of Eton College record the payment "To Glover and his Laborer for two daies brekinge downe Images and filling the places with stone and Plaister." . . . Images were condemned at length in the official *Homilie against peril of Idolatrie* issued in 1563. Their place in the church would now be filled by scriptural verses painted on the walls and altar cloths, and by the literary monuments of the Reformation, the English Bible and Foxe's *Book of Martyrs*.[9]

Gilman goes on to observe that even the ceremonies of the English royal court became less ornate later in the reign of Henry VIII.

One William Dowsing, one of the above mentioned Royal Visitors, records in his diary:

> Stoke-Nayland, Jan. the 19th. We brake down an 100 superstitious pictures; and took up 7 superstitious Inscriptions on the

Grave-Stones, *ora pro nobis*, &c. Barham, Jan. the 22nd. We brake down the 12 Apostles in the Chancel, and 6 superstitious more there; and 8 in the Church, one a Lamb with a Cross X on the back; and digged down the [altar] Steps...[10]

A sense of iconoclasm is discernable, according to Gilman, even in the English literature of the mid-sixteenth century. Writing became less imaginative and more prosaic, mirroring the ascendancy of a word-centered over an image-centered theological climate and also reflecting the "deep suspicion of the idolatrous potential of the fallen mind and its fallen language."[11]

Word Painting in Daniel

Another experience of right-brained worship at Salisbury caught me quite by surprise. It came, of all places, while I was hearing Scripture readings from the book of Daniel. As I was attending multiple daily cathedral services at Salisbury, I heard the appointed Scripture readings day after day; I was reminded that the rhythms of cathedral worship life are similar to those of monastic worship life. The whole point of the multiple monastic services throughout the day was and is to be in constant prayer, praise, and instruction in the Word. This monastic life was seen as the *opus Dei,* the work of God. The appointed Old Testament readings while I was in Salisbury were from the book of Daniel. Each day my fellow worshipers and I heard anew a lengthy episode from that ancient saga. As I sat there at Eucharist and evensong day after day, hearing Daniel's story slowly unfold, the meticulous detail and repetitiousness of the account became increasingly obvious—and humorous:

King Nebuchadnezzar made an image of gold, ninety feet high and nine feet wide, and set it up in the plain of Dura in the province of Babylon. Then he summoned the satraps, prefects, governors, advisers, treasurers, judges, magistrates and all the other provincial officials to come to the dedication of the image he had set up. So the satraps, prefects, governors, advisers, treasurers, judges, magistrates and all the other provincial officials assembled for the dedication of the image that King Nebuchadnezzar had set up, and they stood before it.

Then the herald loudly proclaimed, "This is what you are commanded to do, O peoples, nations and men of every language: as soon as you hear the sound of the horn, flute, zither, lyre, harp, pipes and all kinds of music, you must fall down and worship the image of gold that King Nebuchadnezzar has set up. Whoever does not fall down and worship will immediately be thrown into a blazing furnace."

Therefore, as soon as they heard the sound of the horn, flute, zither, lyre, harp, and all kinds of music, all the peoples, nations and men of every language fell down and worshiped the image of gold that King Nebuchadnezzar had set up.

At this time some astrologers came forward and denounced the Jews. They said to King Nebuchadnezzar, "O king, live forever! You have issued a decree, O King, that everyone who hears the sound of the horn, flute, zither, lyre, harp, pipes and all kinds of music must fall down and worship the image of gold, and that whoever does not fall down and worship will be thrown into a blazing furnace. But there are some Jews whom you have set over the affairs of the province of Babylon—Shadrach, Meshach and Abednego—who pay no attention to you, O king. They neither serve your gods nor worship the image of gold you have set up."

Furious with rage, Nebuchadnezzar summoned Shadrach, Meshach and Abednego. So these men were brought before the king, and Nebuchadnezzar said to them, "Is it true, Shadrach, Meshach and Abednego, that you do not serve my gods or worship the image of gold I have set up? Now when you hear the sound of the horn, flute, zither, lyre, harp, pipes and all kinds of music, if you are ready to fall down and worship the image I have made, very good. But if you do not worship it, you will be thrown immediately into a blazing furnace. Then what god will be able to rescue you from my hand?"

Daniel 3:1-15

What a marvelous riot of redundancy! One evening I was honored to be invited by the cathedral organist to join him in the organ loft for evensong. As one of these readings from Daniel went on at length, he busied himself with all the music-arranging and organ stop-pulling that organists must do. I didn't think he was paying

much attention to the reading until finally he stole a quick glance at me with a twinkle in the corner of his eye and whispered, "I think I've lost the plot!"

It is easy and probably typical for most of us to skim over these flowery repetitions when we read them to ourselves. That is probably what you did as you read it above. We want to get on with it. We don't want to lose the plot. But what an experience it was to hear these accounts read formally, without any attempt at abridgement or haste! I had never previously heard so much of Daniel read so formally. I was reminded that this is how such books were originally intended to be used. They were formally read aloud to groups of listeners. I found part of myself feeling alternately restless or amused. But then I became aware of having another reaction: there was a lilt, a rhythm to these repetitions, which were in their own way something like the calming undulations of the arches in the cathedral nave. They were almost hypnotic.

Then I realized that these slow-paced repetitions gave me ample opportunity to paint a detailed and vivid picture in my mind. I had time to imagine satraps as opposed to prefects, as opposed to governors, as opposed to advisers. I could see the whole lot of them standing—no, kneeling before the image of gold that Nebuchadnezzar had made. I could see in my mind's eye the different instruments—horns, flutes, zithers, lyres, harps, pipes among many others—and imagine what that musical concoction must have sounded like. The story came alive. As I relaxed and let the story have its way with me, I soon realized that this was a story written more for our imaginations (right brain) than for the logic in the plot (left brain). I learned yet another way in which the written Word of God is a marvelously varied gift upon which we are meant to feast with all our minds.

The Influence of the Gathered Community in Worship

Human experiences of fellowship and belonging are exceedingly complex, and I do not believe science is yet ready to tell us exactly where such qualities and feelings are processed in our brains. But

issues of community are absolutely central to true Christian worship and strongly related to nonverbal communication. We speak to each other through our body language, facial expressions, handshakes and hugs, by how we look as we worship together, and even by how our seating is arranged. My time in England also reminded me afresh of why God has instructed us to worship regularly in community.

Not many people attend daily services in a cathedral. The 7:30 a.m. Eucharists attracted roughly 10 to 15 people, who gathered in one of the side chapels in the cathedral. Evensongs drew around 30. Salisbury in November is not much of a tourist center, so those in attendance were largely local folk who came for reasons different from those of most tourists. Evensong is the Anglican answer to the ancient monastic services of vespers and compline. These were traditionally prayer services focusing largely on the corporate praying of the psalms and canticles, as evensong does also.

With so few people in attendance at evensong, it was easy to observe most of one's fellow worshipers, especially since these services take place in the choir area of the cathedral—the enclosed elevated space toward the front of the cathedral, just beyond the nave. The choir area is actually a building within a building, with two ornate wooden walls on either side. Usually about four rows of terraced pews line this long enclosure. The choir occupies the front portion of these pews, members facing one another across the central aisle, and other worshipers occupy the remaining seating, closer to the high altar. People did truly seem to be actively involved in the prayers, readings, hymns, and anthems. These were indeed times of worship for me as I joined the others in prayer and meditation.

I gained further insights about the worshiping community the following week as I attended daily evensongs at various colleges of Cambridge University. Most English college chapels are designed like the choir portion of a cathedral. The typical English college choir has about 30 singers. More often than not, there were more people in the choir than in the congregation. King's College is by far the most famous, both because of the grandeur of its famous chapel and because its choir of men and boys has an international

The choir area of Salisbury Cathedral showing the split choir stalls facing each other.[12]

reputation. But even there the attendance was often very low. At a eucharistic evensong I attended at Clare College, only five or six of us were in the congregation. As at Salisbury, I found I formed certain bonds with the others when there were so few worshipers, especially as I needed to watch others closely for cues as to what to do next.

Attendance picks up quite dramatically at a weekend evensong at King's College, but other colleges seem never to attract many people. As the crowds increased at King's, it seemed that the quality of worship decreased, at least for me. I could tell from their conversations that many of those in attendance were tourists. As the evensong progressed, I noticed a restlessness in the crowded chapel. People were fidgeting with their shopping bags and cameras, whispering to their neighbors, and straining their necks to look all around. Many were not actively involved in saying the prayers or the creed. It felt to me as though many were there merely to see the show and not to participate in worship. At least in part because of the weakness of my own faith, I found it difficult to concentrate on the worship of God in such an environment. I felt alone as a worshiper even in that crowded space.

Immediately after one such crowded evensong at King's College, I hastened to St. John's College Chapel for its evensong. St. John's had the same small number in attendance I had observed all week. Across the aisle from me was a young man sitting by himself in the place where the Scripture readers usually sat. He looked to be of college age. Interested college students, it seems, are chosen to read the appointed Scripture passages, and as it turned out, he was one such student. I could tell by his reading that he was not English but Irish. As he was pretty much in my direct field of vision, I could not help but notice the intensity of his participation through all aspects of the service. His effect upon me was profound. After I had just come from the large semi-involved crowds at King's College, this young man silently communicated to me a humble, devout piety which made it much easier for me to focus on worship, and I felt less alone. By the power of his apparent sincerity of prayer and genuine praise, he ushered me into the presence of the Almighty. May God bless his Irish heart, whoever he is.

This young man helped me realize anew how important is the spiritual intensity of any congregation. Many observers and authors remind us that the most powerful witness to the truth of the gospel in any service of worship is the attitude of the congregation. Members of the current generation of youth in particular are looking for a worship experience marked by a certain passion of commitment—not just from the leaders but more especially from the congregation. It is not so much the friendliness or animation of the congregation that makes the difference, but the corporate sense that these people are serious about their worship. In such a congregation, their praise may not necessarily be loud or exuberant, but it is clearly genuine. Their prayers may not necessarily be long or flowery, but they emanate from the heart. In short, these people are serious about God and each other; they mean business. Such a congregation has established a synergy, a tradition of mutual encouragement and edification that feeds on itself and nourishes not only the members but visitors as well. And such worship can be immensely attractive, convicting, and thus, evangelistic. I am not sure that this is necessarily a right-brain or left-brain issue, but it does fall under the category of nonverbal communication and therefore is appropriate to our subject.

Proceeding with Caution

We have now examined the nature of cerebral cognition, the way it has manifested itself in Scripture, in theology, and throughout history. Along the way, we have already seen some of the practical applications of this study to matters of corporate worship. We have also begun to see some of the worship traditions and attitudes that can stand in the way of a more holistic worship experience. Before making our final recommendations, we are well advised to consider a number of practical issues that can and do stand as roadblocks to achieving balance.

Questions for Thought and Discussion

1. Describe the various church buildings in which you have worshiped. Discuss the details of each.
2. Review the descriptions of medieval churches given in this chapter. What does the architecture of the churches you described in question 1 communicate about the relationship between the worshiper and God?
3. Have someone read aloud the Daniel account discussed in this chapter. Allow time for the story to "have its way with you." Discuss your reactions.
4. Discuss times in your worship experiences when nonverbal communication by and with others has left you feeling alone or isolated from others. Do such situations draw you to worship or does the isolation from others inhibit your ability to worship? Explain.

Chapter Eight

Roadblocks to Holistic Worship

We demolish arguments and every pretension that sets it-self up against the knowledge of God, and we take captive every thought to make it obedient to Christ.
—2 Corinthians 10:5

Until the age of digital keyboards, no one had ever devised a way to construct a keyboard musical instrument that would be perfectly in tune in all keys. A string or wind instrument player or a singer can easily adjust a given pitch up or down a little to get it right in tune. There is no way to give a keyboard instrument this flexibility. Before the time of Johann Sebastian Bach, keyboard instruments were tuned in such a way that they would be perfectly in tune in a few common keys but increasingly out of tune in others as you moved farther away from the common keys. Around the time of Bach, composers and musical theoreticians were working to develop ways of tuning (tempering) keyboard musical instruments, so that they would be able to play satisfactorily in any key. This was called "well-tempered tuning." The compromise was that in so doing, the instruments were not *completely* in tune in *any* key.

J. S. Bach wrote a monumental set of pieces known as *The Well-tempered Clavier* to demonstrate the flexibility of well-tempered tuning. One piece was written for each of the 24 major and minor keys. On a well-tempered keyboard, one could play the entire set without having to retune the instrument. Suddenly, the full spectrum of keys was constantly available to keyboard composers and players. They lost the freshness of accurate tuning, and individual keys lost their unique personalities, but a whole new world of tonal relationships opened and the musical world has never been

the same since. Most people agree that it was a good trade-off, but it was nonetheless a compromise. By now most of our ears are so used to this slight out-of-tuneness that even trained musicians tend not to notice.

There is also such a thing as a well-tempered worship service. It is not a new concept, and most people stand a decent chance of finding at least one in the communities in which they live. Well-tempered worship feeds both sides of the brain in substantial ways. It is not just a matter of having a "blended" service, a term that usually refers merely to a blending of musical styles. Well-tempered worship celebrates the full spectrum of God-given right-brain and left-brain characteristics in all aspects of worship—prayer, praise, word, and sacrament. It involves architecture, acoustics, floor plan, furnishings, and worship order. It has to do with the personality, attitudes, and ethos of the pastor and of each person in the congregation. As with well-tempered music, it involves compromise, and, as in music, not everyone will agree that the areas of compromise are wisely chosen.

Roadblocks to Balance

Let's admit it right up front. Achieving the sort of balance this book calls for is no small task for many churches. Not only does each denomination have its own entrenched ethos, but each congregation within a denomination has its own particular predisposition for a certain sort of worship experience. We all know how much energy it takes to bring about change in most institutions.

What is more, each individual within a congregation has his or her own brain-style signature. If the current minister and a significant number of other decision makers happen to be somewhat right-brained, the challenge just to get a fair hearing for a more left-brained worship encounter grows proportionately.

Such discussions can become heated very quickly. The issue is not merely a matter of culture, ethos, and inertia. Those who have thought through and adopted the biblical and theological perspectives supporting their denominational ethos may well perceive pro-

posed changes in worship style and order to be an attack on the very bedrock of biblical worship.

Theological Roadblocks to Balance

Concern about changes in worship is nothing new. One example of many would be Arthur W. Pink, highly regarded early twentieth century Bible scholar and author and champion of classical Puritanism:

> Much of what is termed "worship" today is fleshly rather than spiritual, and is external and spectacular, rather than internal and reverential. What are all the ornate decorations in our churchhouses for? The stained glass windows, the costly hangings and fittings, the expensive organs! . . .
>
> Worship, then, is the occupation of the heart with a *known* God; and everything which *attracts* the flesh and its sense, *detracts* from real worship. . . . Worship is not by the eyes or the ears, but "in spirit," that is, from the *new nature*. O, how far astray we have gone! Modern "worship" is chiefly designed to render it pleasing to the flesh: "a bright and attractive service," with beautiful surroundings, sensuous music, and entertaining talks. What a mockery and a blasphemy![1]

Many today share his perspective and hold Pink in high regard. Attempts to increase right-brain emphasis in worship generally meet vigorous resistance among worship leaders of this persuasion.

Resistance to balance can come from the other direction as well. We know only too well that much of the impetus for the sixteenth century Reformation came as a reaction to the sorry state of preaching and teaching in the medieval Catholic Church and the resultant biblical and theological ignorance of the average churchgoer. What was needed was some serious left-brained teaching and preaching, rather than mere meditation while the priests muttered in Latin at the high altar half a city block away. The reformers provided that teaching. But the established church fought them with vigor.

Roadblocks to holistic worship can come from both the right and the left of the theological spectrum. Barry Liesch, associate professor of music at Biola University in La Mirada, California, describes the attitudes among some groups of conservative Christians that can hinder balance. He writes:

> I heard the story of a custodian at a Christian college who was cleaning the office of an art instructor. The professor had several of his abstract paintings on the wall and others in progress scattered in different parts of his office. As the custodian cast his eyes at the paintings, he was overheard asking a student incredulously, "This professor of yours—does he talk about God?"[2]

For this conservative layman, abstract art was a sure sign of spiritual decadence.

While serving as minister of music in a Presbyterian church a number of years ago, I used to hold Bible studies in my home. I had a print of Picasso's cubist masterpiece *Three Musicians* hanging on my living-room wall. One evening the group began talking about the painting shortly before we broke for refreshments. After returning from the kitchen, I immediately noticed that the painting had been removed from the wall. One of our more conservative members announced that the painting was degenerate, if not sinful, and took it upon himself to "cleanse" my living room of the grievous impurity. I wondered if there had perhaps been a burning in my absence, but the painting had merely been laid on a bed in my guest room. Of course, most theological conservatives would not want to be considered part of such extremes, but this sort of cynicism remains in some portions of this subculture.

Barry Liesch goes on to address the way some evangelicals tend to esteem propositional statements and to undervalue poetic passages. How tragic! Christian author Dallas Willard, calling for a commitment to the arts, put it poignantly in a chapel service at a Christian college: "I don't want you to think of art as a little frill or whipped cream on the cake of life. It's more like steak and potatoes."

Much of the "steak" in Scripture, including prophecy, comes cast in poetic form. C. S. Lewis disparages people who are on the

lookout for information alone: "As the unmusical listener wants only the Tune, so the unliterary reader wants only the Event." Lewis says: "The most valuable thing the Psalms do for me is to express the same delight in God which made David dance." We need to understand that some metaphors are our only method of reaching a given idea at all.[3]

Other Roadblocks to Balance

We cannot hope to achieve a well-tempered worship service without observing and responding to current cultural trends. What is well-balanced worship for one era is not likely to be as well balanced for another. One of the most pervasive labels for our modern times is *postmodernism*. As a host of writers have been telling us, one of the chief characteristics of postmodernism is the revolution in thinking about truth. Increasingly, people doubt that there is a unified body of truth to be discovered in this world. What is true for one person may not be the truth for another. "You have your truth, I have mine," they say. There is more out there, it is believed, than what can be discerned merely through our five senses.

Thus the door is opened to a host of frankly extrasensory sources for information. There is in all of this a general movement from rationality and objectivity to emotionality and subjectivity. This trend seems to suggest a growing preference for right hemispheric mental functions over left. Some of this tendency has been good for worship; some of it has not. For worship traditions that are too heavily word-oriented, postmodernism can provide some healthy correctives. But where the word is already getting short shrift, it does not appear that the general cultural trend will be of much help in creating better balance.

Worship forms and media that appeal to the right brain are currently popular in many segments of the modern church. There are robust music programs, concert series, liturgical dance troupes complete with banners and streamers, drama companies, and advanced visual and audio technologies. Preaching styles have come a long way since simple expository preaching (verse-by-verse study) or traditional topical sermons. Today preachers use various

narrative or storytelling styles to teach a particular point or truth, as well as first-person sermons in which the preacher speaks as if he or she actually were Moses, Mary, or some other figure. Modern preachers are more likely to share personal experiences from the pulpit. It is common for ministers to forsake the pulpit and to wander among the congregation while preaching, microphone in hand. There is an increased focus on preaching style and technique—the drama of preaching—and high-energy, emotional delivery is considered essential in many pulpits. Even the use of illustrations in sermons is a relatively recent phenomenon and rarely to be found in earlier centuries.

Television, movies, and computers have transformed us into a visual culture. Many churches with "cutting-edge" worship styles focus increasingly on the visual rather than the aural aspects of worship. Worship services get high marks for being techno-savvy.

For many people these days, having an emotional or sensual experience is far more important than learning some truth. Just the other week, while channel surfing late one evening, I stopped for a moment at a channel featuring one of the currently popular TV preachers. His point seemed to be that having an emotional religious experience was more valuable than being able to explain your faith rationally. As he approached the culmination, he abruptly stopped, pointed his finger at the congregation, shook it, and pronounced with great intensity, "A man with an argument is always at the mercy of a man with an experience." The audience/congregation shouted and applauded wildly.

In some Pentecostal or charismatic circles, having a personal encounter or experience with the Holy Spirit is the central aim. While such an encounter might have any combination of right-brain or left-brain elements, the emotional components are largely right-brained. Getting "slain in the spirit," engaging in "holy laughter," jumping and dancing, waving one's arms, or even quietly reveling in the presence of the Lord are all nonverbal, nonrational, and nonlogical (note, I do not say irrational or illogical). Even speaking in tongues, though verbal, is essentially nonrational (some will want to say superrational) in that the speakers generally could not repeat in English what they were saying in tongues. There would appear

to be significant if not primarily right-brain activity in all of these experiences.

I am not ready to claim that any of these emotional experiences necessarily displeases the Lord, but any one or a combination of these manifestations has the potential to become too dominant in a worship service. When such things become the focus to the detriment of sound, rational teaching and preaching, or other more left-brained acts such as affirmations of faith, confessions of sin, or other verbal forms of prayer, the service is as imbalanced as the Puritan service that Arthur Pink promoted.

Evangelical musician and writer Donald Hustad speaks to this concern in his book *True Worship*. He acknowledges that many evangelical churches have come a long way in embracing various art forms in worship, but he fears that a lack of concern for verbal matters is *also* taking root. He faults much of contemporary Christian music for its lengthy repetitions of one or two phrases of sung text. He further notes that the sacrament of the Lord's Supper is often served with few words spoken, and solos and choir anthems are sung without the texts being printed in the bulletin. He summarizes, "Each of these instances gives evidence that cognitive words of biblical truth are not sufficiently important to modern pastors or to congregations, who are content with worship that is more superficially affective than rational."[4]

Achieving balance between right and left sides of the brain can be a challenge in another way. Hustad further observes that in a culture that has little interest in either poetry or theology, the congregational singing of substantial hymnody presents considerable obstacles.[5] Apprehending the meaning of a multi-verse poem has clear benefits but can take significant and sustained mental effort. And as the various books and Web sites addressing the "dumbing down" of America have argued, we are not currently known for our love of mental effort. This may be one reason why so many people prefer repeating a single verse of a praise chorus five times to singing a five-verse hymn. The chorus requires much less theological analysis.

While it may seem that the intent of this book is to promote the exercise of the right brain over the left, that is decidedly not the goal. I am aware that much of my writing is in support of more

right-brain emphasis in worship. Perhaps this seeming bias is because I am a church musician who has spent most of his life chafing under the constraints placed on right-brained worship activities—and not just in matters of music. But many reading these lines will have had the opposite experience. Their worship life may be filled with robust examples of right-brained experiences, but perhaps they have never really been challenged to think logically and systematically about their faith, to know what they believe and why. They may not know the contents of Scripture as well as they should because of a lifetime of sermons and teachings focused on *experiencing* God rather than *understanding* God and his ways. They may not be able to apply biblical principles to the challenges of life because they have not sufficiently applied their left brains to the hard work of developing a personal theology that will stand in life's storms. Merely feeling God's presence or just praising the Lord will not equip an individual to face life's difficulties or to train up children in the nurture and admonition of the Lord.

So we can see that challenges to balanced worship exist on many levels. In making these observations we are beginning to see some of the reasons change often comes so slowly in matters of worship reform.

The Millenial Generation

The postmodern penchant for questioning truth claims is clearly evident in the youngest and newest definable segment of American society, the millenials, or generation Y—those born since 1984. George Barna refers to this generation as the "Mosaics" because "their lifestyles are an eclectic combination of traditional and alternative activities" and "they are the first generation among whom a majority will exhibit a *non-linear style of thinking* [italics added]—a mosaic, connect-the-dots-however-you-choose approach."[6]

"They are," he says, "abundantly comfortable with contradictions. . . . This comfort level is partially a function of their thinking style (i.e., a nonlinear approach, in which any route you take to any end point is equally valid) and partially a reflection of their comfort with diversity and inclusivity."[7] Whereas left-brained ra-

tional, logical, linear thinking was the hallmark of the modernistic Age of Reason or the Scientific Age, Barna suggests we may well be entering an age in which a more holistic right-brained ethos is taking hold. That would not necessarily be any better or worse, but, says Barna, it will be different!

Worship scholar Robert Webber has carefully researched a subsection of this generation, the younger evangelicals.[8] Webber notes differences in how this stratum of society relates to worship as compared to previous generations:

> During the last two decades of the twentieth century, the church growth experts have been saying, "Go contemporary or die," but recently I have been hearing an opposing voice. First of all, some pastors have confided in me that contemporary worship, which is all they have ever known or done, now feels thin, even lifeless and rote. Second, in Christian colleges all over the country students are turning toward a much more quiet worship such as candlelight prayer vespers using Taizé music.

Webber decided to do a survey of students at Wheaton College and Graduate School, involving 176 students in their 20s. He goes on to explain:

> The survey demonstrated some very interesting trends among the younger evangelicals. What they want is a God-centered worship that emphasizes the following nine features:

1. a genuine encounter with God
2. genuine community
3. depth and substance
4. more frequent and meaningful experience of communion
5. challenging sermons and more use of Scripture in worship
6. participation
7. creative use of the senses; visual
8. quiet, characterized by the inclusion of contemplative music and times for quiet personal reflection and intimate relationship with God
9. a focus on the transcendence and otherness of God[9]

Webber goes on to observe:

> The culture of post-2000 is very different than that of the sixties
> and seventies. It is a culture tired of noise, turned off by phoni-
> ness, sick of glitz, and wary of the superficial. It is a culture search-
> ing for an authentic encounter with God, longing for depth and
> substance, craving quiet and spiritual contemplation and moved
> by visual, tactile forms of communication.[10]
>
> Pragmatists [of the past generation], with their seeker-sensi-
> tive movement, missed the heart of the media revolution. They
> rejected symbol, sign, metaphor, imagination, and atmosphere,
> and failed to mine Christian symbolism in space, environment,
> Christian year, art, and most crucially the symbolic power of bap-
> tism and the Eucharist.[11]

Sydney Westrate, one of the younger evangelicals interviewed
in Webber's book, observes: "God seems bigger than words. There
are times when words can't adequately express what we want to
say . . . as we communicate with God, we should not disregard the
nonverbal, but instead embrace it."[12]

Roman Catholic journalist Colleen Carroll Campbell documents
similar trends within the Roman Catholic Church in her book *The
New Faithful: Why Young Adults Are Embracing Christian Orthodoxy*.[13] Like Webber, Carroll demonstrates the distinct break
generation Y has made with the immediately preceding generations,
baby boomers and baby busters. And as well, she documents the
clearly right-brained shift in this new generation. She writes of the
experiences of Dieter Zander, one of the young-adult ministers at
the seeker-sensitive megachurch Willow Creek in South Barrington,
Illinois, outside Chicago:

> "It gets old to get pandered to for so long," said Zander, noting
> that services marketed only to young adults strike them as false.
> "There's something inside of them that says, "This is not the way
> it really is."
>
> Zander has since critiqued the model of generation-specific
> services that informed his work at Willow Creek. He now be-
> lieves that youth ministers would fare better if they address the

ideological shift between the rationality-oriented modern converts of yesterday and their mystery-craving postmodern children.

For many young Christians, worship shot through with symbolism and tradition offers an escape from niche-marketed, age-segmented, or strictly didactic church services. It also feeds the generation-X craving for mystery.

Carroll concludes by observing:

> These young believers cling to the hard gospel and holy mysteries. . . . And they gravitate to churches that help them reverence the intimate yet mysterious God to whom they have surrendered their imaginations, and their very lives.[14]

Mystery, imagination, symbolism, sign, metaphor, use of visual and other senses, sacraments, community, encounter with God, mosaic, nonlinear styles of thinking—note the language these observers of young folk are using. Then review the chart of right-brain and left-brain characteristics in chapter 1. There can be no question that postmodernism and generation Y (the mosaics) in particular have a remarkable affinity with the right side of the brain. Perhaps one of the ways to describe the radical shifts taking place in culture at large is a shift from left-brain to right-brain modes of thought.

Evangelicals on the Canterbury Trail

Another phenomenon, far less in the public eye but still significant, bears mentioning at this point. That is the procession of evangelicals and others from churches whose worship life tends to revolve around teaching and preaching to the Anglican, Catholic, and Orthodox communions. A relatively small but steady stream of discontented Christians have been making this pilgrimage for the past few decades. Robert Webber chronicles this trend in his book *Evangelicals on the Canturbury Trail*.[15] Others among these are painter and filmmaker Franky Schaeffer[16] (son of Christian speaker and writer Francis Schaeffer) and Christian author Thomas Howard.[17] They

didn't all make this switch for the same reasons, of course, but most seem to echo concerns similar to those mentioned by generation Y, though many of these pilgrims are much older. Webber lists six aspects of Anglicanism that are often left unfulfilled by evangelicalism:

1. Anglicanism preserves the sense of mystery that rationalistic Christianity (either liberal or conservative) seems to deny.
2. Anglicanism provides an experience of worship that goes beyond either emotionalism or intellectualism.
3. Anglican worship does not shy away from visible and tangible symbols, such as the Sacraments, that can be felt and experienced with the senses.
4. The Anglican Church has a historic identity through being part of a tradition that embraces and identifies with all God's people throughout history.
5. Anglicanism provides an ecclesiastical home growing out of that historic identity.
6. The Anglican tradition fosters a holistic perspective on spirituality.[18]

Webber writes of his years in various evangelical settings:

> I didn't know it at the time, but I was being swept away into evangelical rationalism, into a proof-texting Christianity, into a Christianity based on scientific enquiry. Christianity was no longer a power to be experienced but a system to be defended.
>
> I was afraid to admit my feelings to anyone else, and I scarcely acknowledged what was happening to my soul. I was drying up spiritually. The reservoir of God's presence in my life was running low. But forget that. It really didn't matter. I had the answers. And, after all, I had been taught the answers were what made the difference.[19]

Throughout the remainder of the book, Webber goes on to explain how this evangelical mind-set was producing an ever-growing emptiness. After a considerable crisis of faith, he was led to discover that what he needed was not answers about God, but God

himself. This great breakthrough led him, eventually, to the Episcopal Church for the reasons listed above. Note once again the right- and left-brain themes that arise in his account: from left-brained rationalism and intellectualism to right-brained mysticism, symbolism, and holistic spirituality.

So we see in how many ways complexities abound. Institutional change of any sort is hard to bring about, especially in tradition-bound organizations like the church. It takes time, patience, and creativity to persuade groups of people to change their ways. Within the church, deeply held theological positions make change especially challenging. It is hard for people (leaders and laity alike) to accept that their beliefs about divine worship may not be as accurate as they thought. Cultural differences add further layers of complexity within denominations and even within congregations. Generational differences seem to be getting more profound all the time. Ethnic differences may manifest themselves. The best of our intentions to bring about a well-tempered worship service will almost certainly run into many if not all of these challenges. This entire web of complexity must be taken into consideration in planning a well-balanced or well-tempered worship service. Keeping in mind these many-faceted considerations related to a well-tempered worship service, let us now proceed to discuss how such a thing might take shape.

Questions for Thought and Discussion

1. Reread the quotation by Pink concerning worship. Does visual imagery detract from your worship of God? Does music? Describe "worship in the Spirit" for you.
2. Think through your personal theology regarding your knowledge of God, each member of the Trinity, humankind, sin, redemption, and life after death. Practice with someone giving an apologetic for your faith.
3. Think about the nine features of worship Webber says Millennials seek and the preferences of both Millennials and people of other generations whom you know. How do their preferences for worship compare with those on Webber's list?

4. In your faith journey, have you found yourself seeking answers, as Webber describes, or rather God's presence? How have the worship styles you have experienced contributed to either of these searches?

Chapter Nine

The Well-Tempered Worship Service

Love the Lord your God with all your heart and with all your soul and with all your mind.

—Matthew 22:37

Having explored all the issues presented in this book, we are finally ready to flesh out in detail the elements of a well-tempered worship service. As we will see, achieving holistic worship does not require the loss of the unique characteristics of a denomination, but it may well require a reevaluation of some denominational or congregational tendencies. Some congregations would probably require considerable alteration to their worship services truly to meet all the needs of their worshipers as presented in this book. I know also that many congregations are already doing excellent work in providing holistic worship to their congregations. Let us now explore some of the major elements of a well-tempered worship service.

Word and Sacrament

Well-tempered worship honors Word and Sacrament equally.

Perhaps the central and most crucial aspect of well-tempered corporate worship is the regular balanced diet of Word and Sacrament. Though the Word will generally focus more on the left brain and the sacraments on the right, both of them can and should, when properly done, engage both sides of the brain. Sermons are more than just logic and linear thought; they paint verbal pictures, engage our imaginations, and excite our emotions. The sacraments are more than symbols; they cannot, in fact, be rightly observed without the use of words.

It is hoped that chapters 3 and 5 adequately demonstrated the biblical call for parity between Word and Sacrament. The model from Scripture, from the early church, and from the reformers is for the Lord's Supper to be a regular part of each weekly service of worship. The first thing any church can do to achieve better balance is to move closer to weekly celebration of the Lord's Supper.

The issue here is not merely the frequency of celebration but also the quality, as discussed in chapter 5. Since the vast majority of Protestants worship in churches where the typical service does not include the Lord's Supper, communion liturgies often seem to be mere add-ons to the regular service, not an integral part of it. The continuing pressure most of us face to complete the entire service in one hour lends a certain air of restlessness and haste to the sacramental proceedings. I believe that this time pressure is one of the main reasons so many pastors hesitate to use the full liturgies recommended by their denominations.

But when sacramental liturgies are not radically abridged, when people are given adequate time and opportunity truly to "make Eucharist" (give thanks), and when ample time and opportunity are allowed to consider the theological implications of baptism and the rich biblical symbolism of water—in short, when the sacraments are treated as the central worship acts that they are, they will not seem to be attachments to normal worship, but will be the heart of worship. And in such settings the Spirit of God is free to move with greater power.

Symbolism

Well-tempered worship values symbolism.

We have observed that every congregation uses symbolism in its worship. It is virtually impossible not to. One can hardly place a piece of furniture in a worship space without creating some sort of symbolic meaning to that placement. Even if we do arrange things for functional reasons, the placement can, over time, take on meanings that were not necessarily intended—sometimes enriching us and sometimes not. The raised platforms for the ministers may make them easier to see *and* elevate their status. Arranging pews in rows

facing the altar and pulpit might best fit the size and shape of the room but further suggest—or symbolize—a certain relationship between leaders and congregation and between the various members of the congregation. God created our brains in such a way that we can hardly help assigning meanings even to seemingly neutral objects. So the issue is not whether to use symbolism but how best to utilize it. A simple procedure might be to list the attributes of worship that are believed to be most important and then to analyze the worship room to see in what ways the architecture and furnishings reinforce or work against those goals.

There is symbolic meaning, as was said, for nearly every furnishing in a worship space. But most worship spaces also have many objects that are clearly and intentionally symbolic: flags; banners; crosses; pictures; designs or even stories in stained-glass windows; flowers; candles; open Bibles on pulpits or tables; designs carved in pulpits, doors, and pews; choir and clergy vestments; textile hangings and paraments; liturgical colors; Christmas or Easter decorations; architectural design; seating for pastors; and congregational seating design.

Then there are symbolic acts that involve our bodies: kneeling in prayer, standing, genuflecting, dancing, prostrating, applying ashes to foreheads, lifting up hands, holding hands, folding hands, shaking hands, and laying on hands. We smell the communion bread and wine, the Easter lilies, the Advent greenery, or the incense.

Each of these speaks its own nonverbal "word," adding multiple layers of meaning to our acts of worship. Likely no church uses all of these, but neither should any church fail to use a significant number of them. And whatever symbolism is intended should be carefully explained and honored. Symbols that are not understood will not speak clearly. Symbols that are *mis*understood can cause confusion or even chaos. Often people have little idea of the meaning of many symbolic features of their worship spaces. For example, my church uses various religious symbols called *crismons* to decorate our church Christmas tree. (For example, circles represent eternity, triangles represent the Trinity, and a chalice represents the Lord's Supper.) Although their meaning has often been explained, we generally hear each year from someone who thanks us for the explanation, saying, for example, "I never knew that

before." We hear the same thing as we regularly explain the meaning of Advent and our Advent wreath. How much explanation is too much? That's for each congregation to decide—but generally, I believe much more explanation of symbolism is in order.

Further, symbols must be honored; that is, taken seriously. For example, careful planning may be necessary if we want symbolic elements to speak to their full potential. What is done must be done with all the excellence, love, insight, knowledge, and skill that can be brought to bear. We must not hide our symbolic lights under a bushel basket. If one is going to use fresh bread for communion, choose a bread whose aroma fills the room. Since placing a covering over the elements is often no longer necessary (few churches still have open windows that allow flies to get to the bread and wine), they can remain uncovered, allowing the aroma of the bread and even the wine to permeate the room. If one is not immersing at baptism, see to it that the water is not underplayed. Pour it from a pitcher into a bowl. Make noise with it. Let the water run down your arm. Don't be afraid to make things wet. It's just water. It will dry. If you are standing to say the Creed, stand tall. If you are creating a banner, design one that will remind the congregation of something truly important, and craft it in such a way that it catches one's attention for its message—not for its shoddy construction. In well-balanced worship, we value and make full use of symbols.

Spoken Word

Well-tempered worship values the spoken word.

Even the most perfectly balanced service of worship will be filled with spoken words. This is as it should be, as it must be. But we have noted that verbalization is not an exclusively left-brained function. While words can be used to build a sequence of left-brained logic, they can also set a mood, fire our imaginations, or paint a picture. This is done in at least two ways—by *what* is said and by *how* it is said.

Left-brain style preachers may have trouble remembering to include enough illustrations in their sermons. Their natural proclivity for developing a solid line of logic often gives them a strong,

even exclusive bias in favor of verse-by-verse expository preaching[1] or other styles favored by logic-based thinkers. They may overfocus on delivering information about the Bible or God at the expense of explaining how the dogma actually helps us live our lives. Such preachers may equate knowing about God with knowing God. Their penchant for sequential detail requires disciplined concentration from their listeners.

Right-brain style preachers are likely to feel a certain degree of reticence about simply developing biblical or theological competence in themselves and their congregations. They might tend to paint word pictures with broad strokes and let the people draw their own conclusions. Their congregations may listen with rapt attention from the first word to the last as they masterfully spin one illustration, one imaginative account after another. But if such pastors are not careful, their congregations may not be equipped with the basic biblical and theological knowledge necessary to deal with real-life issues.

Both preaching styles are likely to have an enthusiastic camp of supporters as well as a restless corps of critics—a division based, in part at least, upon the right-brain or left-brain styles of the various listeners. Of course, there will always be a rather large group of church members who are neither particularly right-brain nor left-brain dominant. They will be better able to adapt to and benefit from either preaching style.

The point is that preachers need to be sure that they are feeding *all* the members of their congregations. Pastors with no strong hemispheric dominance are likely to draw naturally upon both sides of the brain for sermon material and style. Thus there is likely to be something for everyone in their sermons over time. They may preach expository sermons as well, but they are more likely to include right-brain elements.

But to the degree that preachers favor one hemisphere over the other, to that same degree they must struggle to achieve greater balance, not only in preaching but also in other areas of worship leadership.

Anyone can exercise the weaker side of the brain and strengthen it simply by engaging regularly in mental activities directed to the weaker hemisphere. But for those with a strong preference for one

side, the use of the other side will not be as enjoyable, nor will it be as efficient. But preachers are obligated to find methods of preaching that over time, at least, will have meaning for all their listeners. That's their pastoral duty. Listeners in the congregation are obligated to find ways to stay engaged with the sermon, even when it is directed to their weaker cerebral hemisphere. That is their duty.

Content aside, much balance can be maintained in public speaking by considering elements of diction, timing, and style—the *way* one uses words. The very manner in which one speaks communicates as much as the bare meaning of the words, sometimes more. One can speak of the love of God, but if one's tone of voice communicates anger or condemnation, the hearers will "hear" the anger rather than the spoken words of love.

Here's another example: if the rate of speed is too fast, listeners may assume that the speaker is nervous and may become uncomfortable themselves or stop listening altogether. Clean, clear articulation tends to put listeners at ease because it is easier to understand.

Pacing is also important. How long to pause before or after a pivotal point in the sermon, how long to wait between various acts of worship, how quickly the musicians introduce a musical response after a prayer or the offering—all these are important matters of pacing. Concern for such elements is not nit-picking. The pacing does much to set the mood of worship—celebrative, meditative, or sorrowful. The pacing of a funeral service is likely to be slower than that of a wedding. Good Friday will be paced differently from Easter.

Perhaps most important of all in these matters is the issue of style. Style is difficult to define with words, but we know when a speaker's style is effective. It involves diction and pacing but goes beyond them to include tone of voice, choice of words, and dialect or regional accent. For decades Garrison Keillor has mesmerized audiences with his "news from Lake Wobegon" stories on the radio show *A Prairie Home Companion*. It would be difficult to say exactly what makes him such an engaging verbal communicator. One might mention his gentle tone of voice, his sense of timing, his choice of words, or the content and wisdom of the stories themselves. But the cumulative effect is magical.

A lot of this kind of ability is mere gift. But there are steps we can all take to be more engaging public speakers. We can make a

short list of speakers whom we ourselves find engaging and take time to analyze why they have such a positive effect on us. We can electronically record our own public speaking for careful analysis. We can find someone who we know will be honest and get his or her sense of what our style communicates and how it might reinforce or differ from the content of our words.

The public reading of Scripture presents special challenges. If we believe Scripture to be the very Word of God, then its public reading should be taken as seriously as the other elements of worship. The reading of Holy Scripture itself is weightier, more important, than the commentary upon it in the sermon. Yet the public reading of the Scripture often comes off as if the reader had not practiced even one time. Mispronounced words, pauses at the wrong spots, a halting delivery—these not only distract but also get in the way of the listeners' understanding of the text.

Even when the text is accurately read, however, the style of delivery may be weak or hard to follow. Some readers speak in a monotone, resulting in an absence of *any* style. Many if not most use a manner of speech in reading in church that is different from their usual way of speaking. For most this means less expressiveness than they would normally put forth. Some repeat the same pattern of raising and lowering the pitch of their voice for every sentence in a way that has little to do with the meaning of the words. Some habitually emphasize adjectives; others stress the verbs.

The most effective—the most believable—readers I have heard are those who read the passage as if they were giving a personal account of what they themselves have just heard or seen. They read as if they have just arrived home and are telling their spouses what they just saw Jesus do, or Elijah, or Mary. They read biblical history as if they were present at the event. They read quotations as if they were saying those words themselves in real life. One must first think: how would I say this if I were just talking normally? This is not easy, since the Scriptures do not generally use the words we would naturally use. So one must practice reading these somewhat alien words to find the way they sound most natural for oneself. And, of course, all this must be done with a mind to communicating a faithful interpretation of the passage. This is oral interpretation; this is exegeting a passage in the act of reading it. Scripture properly read is a sermon already half preached.

It indeed takes practice to read this way, and that means that one must spend ample time preparing to read well. It requires a good translation of the Scriptures, one that reasonably approaches modern American speech. Often one may not study from the same translation from which one reads in public. After all, one of the reasons we have various translations of Scripture is to accommodate differing uses of Scripture.

By carefully considering such elements as pacing, diction, and oral interpretation, one can draw the right brain into the predominantly left-brained domain of verbal skills. Vivid pictures can be painted, the imagination can be aroused, and the matchless beauties of the Word of God can be rightly honored by beauty of delivery. Surely we will want to apply our full minds to the full understanding of the Word of God.

Welcoming the Arts

Well-tempered worship welcomes and nurtures the arts.

Few would wish to argue that music has no place in worship. Of all the arts, music has been the most warmly embraced by the Christian church. Musical controversies today revolve not around a mandate for music in general, but around which musical styles are appropriate for Christian worship. Much has been written on this subject in recent years, and I shall not enter the fray in this book.

Let me simply restate my growing conviction that mere music—music without words—is a valid medium through which God may speak. So often music is seen as an aid to worship rather than as an act of worship itself. Instrumental selections played before and after the service are regarded by many as background music while people are arriving or preparing for worship, and are departing or engaging in fellowship afterward. We even use the words *prelude* and *postlude*, suggesting that these musical selections occur *before* and *after* worship, not as part of it. We live in a culture drenched in music, much of which is labeled background music and never intended to be consciously considered. It is piped into stores, offices, factories, restaurants, restrooms, and elevators. Many

of us have music playing in our homes all day long. We have trained ourselves to ignore it. When in our worship we reinforce these perceptions of music as medium rather than message, we compromise the Spirit's effectiveness to speak through it.

There are other common problems regarding worship music. Every time the worship leader indiscriminately skips stanzas of a hymn, the message is sent that the hymn is not really an important act of worship. It communicates that the flow of meaning from one verse to the next can be disrupted at will, skipping verse 3, or singing just the first and last verses. It doesn't matter; "it's just a hymn." Suddenly the hymn is reduced to a mere tool to create a mood or, worse yet, as a way to separate two prayers or other verbal elements. I might add that though I am using the term "hymns," the same issues naturally hold for congregational metrical Psalms or contemporary songs.

Another way we send subtle messages that we need not pay close attention to music is by placing a choral anthem or vocal solo during the offering. Instead of paying attention to the meaning of the words, silently praying or praising with the singers, the worshipers are busy finding their purses, filling out envelopes, writing checks, watching the ushers, and passing plates.

Well-tempered worship recognizes that music is not a tool to set a mood, but an essential act of worship in itself. Worshipers should be trained to know that God is likely to speak through the music as well as though the words and to *expect* such messages to reach even them.

The Visual Arts in Worship

At a number of points in this book we have discussed the visual arts and their place in worship. Much of the symbolism in a worship space takes the form of visual art. We have further pointed out that humans cannot help but add artistic touches to even the most practical, functional objects—tables, chairs, doors, ceilings. This tendency is interesting in light of the Shakers' commitment to simplicity in general, their understanding of furniture design and function, and their insistence that the furniture not distract from

worship. By designing something so simple, they created furniture of great beauty—which, in a way, was what they sought to avoid! At a basic level, the visual arts are all around us all the time.

We have also emphasized that human creativity is a large part of what it means for us to have been created in the image of God. If Christians are those who by the power of God's Spirit are being restored to the fullness of humanity—life as God intended for us all along—then Christians should be producing truly excellent and enlightened examples of human creativity. The church should be at the forefront in encouraging and fostering these gifts of human creativity, including the visual, aural, and verbal arts.

Nurturing the visual arts in the Christian community means more than merely hanging some pretty pictures here and there. It means more than enriching worship with banners, liturgical dancing, colorful overhead projections, or fancy liturgical vestments. Churches should be actively engaged in developing the creative talents of people among their own membership and beyond. Such activity might include sponsoring art exhibits and workshops, incorporating members' art work in worship bulletins, or providing a scholarship fund for gifted people who could not otherwise afford special instruction. In these ways the church can make a strong statement that such talents are gifts from God and therefore worthy of our full support.

Diversity

Well-tempered worship honors diversity.

In considering the issues raised by this book, we realize there are good reasons that account for the existence of the various Christian denominations. Theological and geographical differences aside, we, in the providence of God, have been created with remarkably different ways of receiving and evaluating information and communicating with each other. It is not that we simply *prefer* one mode of thinking above another. Some of us find that our mental equipment truly *limits* our ability to think in certain ways. As this constraint relates to worship matters, it may not be a matter of

mere stubbornness that we want parts of the service a certain way; we may have true limitations in our ability to adapt to those parts.

It is not surprising that certain of us gravitate to Baptist worship styles and others to Episcopal ones. In addition to theological and cultural issues, right-brain/left-brain styles will give some people a natural proclivity for one or the other. In this regard, we might go so far as to say that denominational differences are at times a good and necessary thing. But what if for other reasons you are committed to a particular denomination? Considering that in any region one is sure to find people exhibiting the full spectrum of cerebral thought patterns, perhaps denominations should work toward providing a variety of worship styles within a given geographical location. In this way people strongly committed to, for example, a Methodist understanding of the faith would not be tempted to leave their denomination to find a way of worship that meets their needs.

But of course, we quickly see that even if denominations provided such diversity in one locale, not everyone's needs would be met. Any congregation, no matter how small, is likely to have among its members people of every imaginable cognitive pattern or style. Even if one were to create a brand-new congregation composed only of left-brained people, soon there would be marriages and children. And even if the church managed to enforce a rule that its members could marry only other left-brained people, they could never require that couples could have only left-brained children! There is no way to get around it. Every congregation will have the inevitable mix of cognitive styles. So it is that each congregation, regardless of denominational, geographical, or cultural setting, must consider how to communicate the gospel and to facilitate the prayers and praises of all its members.

Those in leadership positions must be especially careful to consider the needs of those whose hemispheric preferences differ from their own. The goal must remain, in every instance, to have each person engaged in worship with all his or her mind. This is, frankly, not easy or even likely. It may not even be possible. But, like Christ's challenge to "be perfect as your heavenly Father is perfect," it is still the necessary goal. If a church's leadership remembers that the diversity of its membership is a good gift from God, it can be easier

to maintain a positive attitude toward the challenges diversity always produces.

For example, when a member approaches a worship leader or committee with suggestions on how to improve the church's worship, it is always easy for leaders to dismiss those ideas that do not resonate well in their own minds. Sometimes they may react in this way because the suggestions are truly flawed theologically or practically. At other times excellent suggestions are dismissed simply because of the blindness caused by differing hemispheric preferences. And, as we have seen in earlier chapters, sometimes entire theological traditions can develop ingrained worship patterns that were never as biblically sound as was thought. In such cases new worship ideas can be dismissed on well-intentioned but less-than-solid biblical grounds.

Clearly, the innovations to our worship that a diverse membership might ask for should not be approved without careful theological reflection. Making changes in worship is hard work and takes much time. Many new worship suggestions providentially open doors for fruitful study and learning by leadership groups or Sunday school classes. Such suggestions might even be addressed in a sermon series. Therefore we should not be quick to dismiss new ideas for worship, even questionable ones. Rather than immediately dismissing them as threats, we might welcome them as an opened door to group study and opportunities for learning. But all too often these opportunities for growth are lost either because of emotionally negative knee-jerk reactions or because no one in leadership has the necessary doctrinal foundations in worship to lead meaningful discussions. At other times fear of possible controversy paralyzes any impetus for change, or even discussion about change.

Sometimes helpful ideas are too readily dismissed simply because their historical roots are questionable. For example, many churches today have begun distributing the bread and wine for the Lord's Supper through the means of intinction. With intinction one dips a piece of bread into a common cup of wine or juice, thus taking bread and wine together. Some object to intinction simply because it has not been a part of their tradition. Others have objected to intinction on theological grounds, since it began as a way for Catholics to take Holy Communion in both kinds, rather than

just the bread, while minimizing the fear of spilling "Christ's blood." The Catholic connection is a problem for some Protestants, and the de-emphasis on the cup is a problem for others. It is true that intinction has its faults. It blurs the "meal" aspects of the Lord's Supper, minimizes the emphasis on Christ's blood, and strikes some as unsanitary, since many fingers can make contact with the contents of the chalice. Besides, it makes the bread soggy.

Yet, for those who object to partaking from a common cup for sanitary reasons, intinction can be a helpful compromise. Intinction has a way of focusing our attention on the one loaf and one cup (1 Cor. 10:16, 17), an extremely important biblical aspect of the Lord's Supper that is utterly confounded by our use of individual servings. So our main point is, if one is to dismiss intinction or some other worship practice, do so for a better reason than merely that its historical roots are tainted.

Jesus prayed fervently that the church would be one (John 17). It is as if he knew that God's gift of human diversity would also be the source of some of our greatest challenges. Our growing awareness of right-brain/left-brain issues helps us understand some of the underlying reasons for our diversity. Our unity and wholeness as the body of Christ can only be enriched by a continued openness to worship that engages the whole mind.

Prayer

Well-tempered worship encourages various forms of prayer.

Over the years of my teaching career I have been surprised to discover how many Christians struggle with their prayer lives. This is true even for seminarians, more than one might realize. It comes as a relief to many Christians to discover that there are quite a few different ways to pray, including normal conversation, praying the Psalms, reading or writing prayers, and silent meditation, among others. Although I would not be willing to assign specific types of prayer as necessarily right- or left-brained, it seems clear that different prayer formats would engage different parts of the brain.

I have a friend who has difficulty focusing her mind when she is seated or still. Frankly, corporate worship on a Sunday morning is

a challenge for her, even though she is in a leadership role at a church. It requires a special degree of mental effort for her just to stay tuned in. Personal prayer is difficult for her for the same reason. She has discovered that if she has something to do with her fingers, she can stay focused better. So she went out and bought some beads with which she made a prayer chain. Each bead represents a different person or prayer concern. With these beads, she can settle herself into a meaningful prayer time. Shall we tell her to cease this practice because it's not very Protestant? Not I. I do not know whether this is a right-brain/left-brain issue, but clearly, the beads activate some different part of her brain, and the result is a much improved prayer life.

Some churches and municipalities are installing labyrinths on their grounds. A labyrinth is different from a maze. A maze contains numerous dead ends and only one way to get through. The successful navigation of a maze requires vigorous exercise of the left brain. One must remember past wrong turns and devise strategies to get through. A labyrinth has similar twists and turns, but only one path that inevitably leads one to the center and back out again. No strategy or memory is necessary. There is no problem to solve. It is simply a metaphor for the spiritual journey or life in general. One approaches it rather passively. Quietly walking through a labyrinth can reduce one's stress level. It can be a means of quieting the mind for purposes of prayer or meditation.

This labyrinth can be seen today on the floor of the Chartres Cathedral in France.[2]

Again, many Christians will have an immediate reaction against such a spiritual aid because it reminds them of the New Age movement or other non-Christian spiritualities. And it is certainly true that some people in these movements make use of labyrinths. But so did the medieval Christian church. The cathedral in Chartres, France, still has a labyrinth on its floor that was constructed around 1200.

My point is not to suggest that more churches should build labyrinths or sell prayer beads but to demonstrate the different ways the human mind can work. For some, sitting still and praying is no problem. Others, and not just children, may need devices that help them gain access to different parts of the brain. Some people may seek God's guidance about a problem by active problem-solving strategies, while others need to quiet their minds in order to hear God's still, small voice. The larger truth is that we all need to draw on a greater diversity of ways to use our minds in worship and elsewhere. At any rate, we all need to be careful about too quickly passing judgment on spiritual practices that do not automatically seem useful to us, or which might even seem theologically questionable at first. We may be denying others the only means by which their God-given brains can process information or experience. Currently a great deal is being written about how physical action adds to the brain's power. A quick Internet search on this topic will yield much information.

Welcoming the Children

Well-tempered worship remembers the children.

Finally, a word must be said about children in worship. Jesus said, "Let the little children come to me, and do not hinder them" (Matt. 19:14). Yet many of our worship services hinder children in all sorts of ways. We all know about the short attention spans of children and how easily they can become restless. We remember what we ourselves did in church services as children to pass the time. We were too young to comprehend intellectually what was happening around us, but there were parts of the experience that caught our attention. Perhaps it was the music, something in the stained-glass windows or banners, or perhaps the tone of the preacher's voice.

The church I attended as a child dedicated a new sanctuary in 1957, so I know my memories of the previous sanctuary come from when I was 4 or 5. What impressions have stayed with me? I remember how big the room seemed. I remember my mother's white gloves. I remember how good the grape juice smelled on Communion Sundays. I remember a set of chimes hanging on a side wall and a balcony over those chimes. I remember the preacher pounding on the pulpit during the sermons and shouting in what seemed an angry voice. What I remember says something about me and something about my church. I am aware that the place has left an impression to this day—and that not all the impressions are positive. An angry voice and a pounding hand are mixed with the pleasant sights, sounds, and smells of that room. I remember being comfortable and contented there (the angry minister was far away up front).

We can be reasonably assured that young children will not remember much of the content of sermons, prayers, or Bible lessons in worship services, but all sorts of other things are sure to make lasting impressions, for good or ill. Thus is molded a child's concept of worship—and of God—from earliest times. Worship rich in godly stimulation for both sides of the brain, but especially the right, is more likely to instill a sense of comfort, pleasure, and belonging in the young—even the very young. What's more, real learning can occur in the young even before their brains are ready for a well-reasoned lesson. They learn from the richness of their environment. They learn from their encounters with other people. And though they may not grasp the meaning of Scripture right away, they can easily store up a repertoire of Bible stories for later reference and interpretation. We are all captivated by a good story. It stimulates our imaginations, enlivens us, and teaches us about life on planet earth. Stories also teach us about God. In chapter 2, C. S. Lewis reminded us that stories do more than teach us *about* God; they have the potential to let us *experience* God.

The Bottom Line

It has been our task in this book to explore the ways God has filled his Word, his world, and the entire universe with vast and varied

modes of communication. We have seen how he has endowed us with the mental equipment needed to take part in this cosmic conversation. We have noted how Scripture gives ample evidence of God's consistency in speaking though all these modes. We have seen how it requires all five of our senses and more to apprehend all that God is saying to us. And we have attempted to draw out specific ramifications for Christian worship.

The message of this book can be summarized in the following points:

1. *God has given each of us certain predispositions in the way we use the two hemispheres of our brains.* Some people are rather balanced in their use of both sides; others have a more-or-less marked preference for one side over the other. God made us this way. Therefore, we have a sort of creation mandate to honor and accommodate the full spectrum of these thought patterns in our worship services. In so doing we ensure that no one is regularly handicapped in participating in prayer and praise, Word and Sacrament. We further honor this mandate by remembering that having a preference for modes of thought from one hemisphere does not excuse us from using our other hemisphere, even though it is harder work to do so. There are no circumstances under which a portion of our God-given minds should be allowed to remain fallow. Such minds miss much of what God is saying. This can never be a good thing.

2. *Each congregation will always contain among its members the full spectrum of cerebral styles and patterns of thought.* Marriages, births, and new members are sure to introduce diversity. Yet, it cannot be ignored that some denominations have an ethos that favors one side of the brain over the other. To a certain degree, this characteristic is not a bad thing, since it is so difficult to construct a worship service that will be equally conducive to all stylistic types. It is a blessing that people can find denominations especially equipped to minister in ways that best fit the ways their brains work. It is also wise in a given location to plant churches of various worship styles within a given denomination. Therefore points 1 and 2 must be kept in a certain dynamic tension.

3. *We need each other.* Left-brained people have insights and understandings that right-brained folk would never notice and vice versa. Just as the *Imago Dei* can be expressed fully only when men and women work together, so the work of the church cannot be

fully envisioned and enacted without the mutual cooperation of the full spectrum of cerebral stylistic patterns. But, as always, the gift of diversity comes with the usual challenges and frustrations.

4. *Trends function like a pendulum, with reaction and counter-reaction.* Sanity, or at least balance, generally lies somewhere in the middle of the pendulum swing. But balance is rather hard to define in matters of right-brain/left-brain issues. What feels like balance to one may seem incredibly one-sided to another. This difference in perception is often not an indication that anything is amiss, but simply a manifestation of the diversity of creation. So an understanding of and appreciation for this diversity can avert many an argument, misunderstanding, and controversy.

5. *It is surprisingly easy for one's theology of worship to be influenced by cerebral stylistic preferences.* Many people's negative reactions to ceremony or symbolism, or to a particular preaching or teaching style, are not always as purely theological as they might think. Their reactions may be influenced by an inability to appreciate right-brained concerns. Similarly, many right-brain-leaning folk react negatively to their pastors or teachers, or at least to their sermons, lessons, or worship style, because these lay members have more difficulty processing left-brained patterns of thought. How easily we assume the purity and integrity of our theological positions! And armed with an arrogant sureness that we "have the mind of Christ" in a given matter, we enforce a worship regimen that seems right to us because it *feels* right to us, and to those other like-minded writers we have been studying. It would make an interesting study to see how many of those who positively influence us in such matters share similar cerebral thought patterns with us.

6. *We live in a postmodern age that reveres feelings and sensual experience but has little expectation of ever knowing ultimate truth.* The church matches this blindness with its own if we react by running away from feelings and the sensual. One does not correct an imbalance by creating an inverse imbalance.

7. *God's abolition of the Old Testament ceremonial law in the present New Testament era by no means implies his rejection of the right side of the brain.* It is the sacrificial system that was abrogated—not ceremony, symbolism, color, or music. God desires worship that engages our whole mind.

8. *According to Scripture and all the major reformers, the normative weekly service of worship should always include the Lord's Supper.* Nonetheless, I continue to find wide-scale resistance to weekly communion celebrations among the vast majority of Protestants. I think some of this resistance could be overcome with some solid teaching and preaching about the meaning of the sacraments. Quicker methods of distributing the elements can often make the celebration more time-efficient, a change that can meet other objections.

9. *It is one thing to know a lot of information about God and another actually to know God or experience God.* Simply to teach doctrine about God is not yet to engage in full Christian worship. True Christian corporate worship must consistently focus on both teaching truth and enabling an encounter with the living God. The former does not necessarily lead to the latter.

Thanks be to God, there are churches in many denominations that do quite well in addressing most if not all of these nine issues. Seeing how the modern worship renewal movements have been around for nearly 50 years now, we should well expect to see significant fruit, and indeed, these movements have produced much good fruit. But it is my observation that there remain many churches in many denominations whose worship practices lean precariously in one direction or the other. As has been noted, it is no small matter to bring about changes in congregations, let alone in denominational traditions. But on the other hand, everything that lives experiences change.

Charles Wesley's great hymn *Love Divine, All Loves Excelling* climaxes on a theme of change, and change on a grand scale:

> Changed from glory into glory, till in heaven we take our place,
> Till we cast our crowns before thee, lost in wonder, love, and
> praise.

I can only hope that some of the observations presented in this book will be useful in promoting change of this sort—wholesome and holistic worship, worship that engages our beings so fully that we actually lose ourselves in the wonder of that God who comes to us and speaks to us on so many levels. May we all rejoice in all

God's good gifts, one of the greatest of which is to worship the Lord our God not only with all our hearts but also with all our minds.

Questions for Thought and Discussion

1. List the attributes of worship that you believe to be most important.
2. Analyze the space in which you most often worship to see in what ways the architecture and furnishings reinforce or work against those attributes.
3. Practice alone and with your discussion group reading one or two passages of Scripture. Using the criteria the author discusses, evaluate how effectively you communicate the meaning of the passage.
4. What are your habits of prayer? Comment on the author's suggestions regarding aids to encourage focus during prayer times, whether corporate or individual.
5. Discuss one or two insights you have gained from reading this book that would help you plan or participate in worship in the future.

Notes

Introduction

1. This is Webber's basic thesis in his book *The Younger Evangelicals: Facing the Challenges of the New World* (Grand Rapids: Baker, 2002).
2. The questions for thought and discussion found at the end of each chapter were provided by M. Jerdone Davis, director of the Christian education program at Erskine Theological Seminary.

Chapter 1, The Human Brain

1. Photo obtained with the permission of Paul Pietsch, professor emeritus, School of Optometry, Indiana University, www.indiana .edu/~pietsch/callosum.html (accessed March 3, 2004).
2. www.nobel.se/medicine/laureates/1981/ (accessed October 2004).
3. In general, each hemisphere of the brain controls the opposite side of the body, including, legs, hands, eyes, ears, and perhaps even facial expressions.
4. www.indiana.edu/~pietsch/split-brain.html (accessed October 2004).
5. Information obtained from e-mail interviews conducted by the author with Dr. Purves, June 2005.
6. Information obtained from e-mail interviews conducted by the author with Dr. Ringholz, June 2005.
7. Lateralization refers to situations in which a cognitive function is located primarily in one hemisphere.

Chapter 2, Historical Survey of Holistic Brain Issues

1. Carol Doran and Thomas Troeger, *Trouble at the Table: Gathering the Tribes for Worship* (Nashville: Abingdon, 1992), 107-108.

2. Margaret R. Miles, *Image as Insight: Visual Understanding in Western Christianity and Secular Culture* (Boston: Beacon Press, 1985), 103.

3. Albert Blackwell, *The Sacred in Music* (Louisville: Westminster John Knox, 1999), 43.

4. Plato, *Republic* 531a, trans. Paul Shorey (London: William Heinemann, 1969), 191-193.

5. Oliver Strunk, *Source Readings in Music History* (New York: W. W. Norton, 1950), 26-27.

6. Dom Gregory Dix, *The Shape of the Liturgy* (New York: Seabury, 1945), 24.

7. If this was their attempt, they failed. The surviving artwork at that synagogue is said to be of a much higher quality.

8. I am indebted to Janet R. Walton, *Art and Worship: A Vital Connection* (Collegeville, Minn.: Liturgical Press, 1988), 19-29, for much of the information about Dura-Europos.

9. Don G. Campbell, *Introduction to the Musical Brain*, 2nd ed. (St. Louis: MMB Music, Inc, 1992).

10. St. Augustine, *The Confessions of St. Augustine* (New York: Washington Square Press, 1951), 200-203.

11. *St. Augustine on the Psalms*, vol. 2, trans. Dame Scholastica Hebgin and Dame Felicitas Corrigan (New York: Newman Press, 1961), 111-112. The *Jubilus* has a long and revered tradition. Many believe that the "spiritual songs" mentioned by St. Paul in Ephesians 5:19 and Colossians 3:16 refer to a sort of nonverbal cantillation sung under the direct influence of the Holy Spirit, perhaps in various states of ecstasy. The *Jubilus* figures prominently in the history of monastic song through the Middle Ages, where it was often applied to the last syllable of the word *alleluia*, especially when that was the final word in the musical phrase. The singer, upon completion of the established tune, continues to improvise upon the final syllable, "*a*," for an extended period of time.

12. Donald Fairbairn, *Eastern Orthodoxy through Western Eyes* (Louisville: Westminster John Knox, 2002), 104.

13. Ibid., 110.

14. Blackwell, *The Sacred in Music*, 91.

15. Walton, *Art and Worship*, 34-35.

16. Ibid., 34-35.
17. David W. Music, "John Newton's Sermons on Handel's *Messiah*," *The American Organist* 37, no. 8 (August 2003): 62.
18. Ibid.
19. C. S. Lewis, "Myth Became Fact," in *God in the Dock: Essays on Theology and Ethics* (Grand Rapids: Eerdmans, 1970), 64.
20. C. S. Lewis, *Surprised by Joy* (New York: Harcourt Brace Jovanovich, 1955), 6.
21. Ibid., 134-136.
22. C. S. Lewis, *Rehabilitations and Other Essays* (New York: Oxford University Press, 1939).
23. Many of the insights in this section come from Colin Duriez in *The C. S. Lewis Encyclopedia* (Wheaton. Ill.: Crossway Books, 2000), particularly his entry on "Imagination."
24. C. S. Lewis, *The Pilgrim's Regress* (Grand Rapids: Eerdmans, 1981), 169.
25. Ghiselin Brewster, ed., *The Creative Process: Reflections on the Invention of Art* (Berkeley: University of California Press), 1996.
26. Taken from the Web page *Heartquotes* at www.heartquotes .net/ Einstein.html (accessed October 25, 2005).
27. D. J. McCormick and C. D. Plugge, "If I Am an Artist, What's Wrong with My Picture?" in "Deeply Rooted, Branching Out, 1972-1997," Annual AEE International Conference Proceedings (Boulder, Colo.: Association for Experimental Education, 1997).
28. T. M. Amabile, *Creativity in Context* (Boulder, Colo.: Westview Press, 1996).

Chapter 3, The Biblical Call for Hemispheric Balance

1. Bruce K. Waltke, with Cathi J. Fredricks, *Genesis: A Commentary* (Grand Rapids: Zondervan, 2001), 80.
2. James Strong, *New Strong's Exhaustive Concordance* (Nashville: Thomas Nelson, 2001), see dictionary at back of concordance, 68, 95.
3. Alan Richardson, *A Theological Word Book of the Bible* (New York: Macmillan, 1950). The entry on 144-145 on the word *Mind* includes, immediately after this word in the heading, the

secondary meaning of *Heart*, indicating the interrelatedness of the two words.

4. A *chiastic* structure, or a *chiasm*, is a compositional form featuring two multisectional structures that form a mirror image of each other, such that the first section corresponds to the last, the second to the second from last, etc. There is generally a crucial pivotal point in the middle that stands alone and underscores the central theme. See Philippians 2:6-11, the famous *kenosis* passage, for a splendid example.

5. Waltke, *Genesis: A Commentary,* 81.

6. Louis Berkhof, *Systematic Theology* (Grand Rapids: Eerdmans, 1953), 203-205.

7. See the New American Standard Version.

8. Strong, *New Strong's Exhaustive Concordance,* dictionary, 75.

9. Christopher A. Hall, "Classical Ear-Training: What the Church Fathers Heard in Homer and Virgil Tuned Them to the Harmonies of Scripture," *Christian History,* vol. XXII, no. 4, 40.

10. Martin Luther, "A Treatise on the New Testament, That Is the Holy Mass" in *Luther's Works* (Philadelphia: Fortress, 1965) 35:8.

11. John Calvin, *The Institutes of the Christian Religion,* ed. John T. McNeill (Philadelphia: Westminster, 1960) book IV, ch. XIV, no. 1, 1277.

Chapter 4, Worshiping with Words

1. Quotation from "Bible Research" Web site www.bible-researcher.com/language-quotes.html (accessed January 10, 2006).

2. Strong, *New Strong's Exhaustive Concordance,* dictionary, 139.

3. Ibid., 76.

4. Ibid., 101.

Chapter 5, Songs, Sacraments, and Symbols

1. Russel Nelson Squire, *Church Music: Musical and Hymnological Developments in Western Christianity* (St. Louis: Bethany Press, 1962), 48.

2. Dietrich Bonhoeffer, *Life Together,* John W. Doberstein, trans. (New York: Harper and Row, 1954), 59.

3. *The Ladies' Library, written by a lady,* published by Richard Steele, 4th ed., 1732. Cited in Quentin Faulkner, *Wiser Than Despair: The Evolution of Ideas in the Relationship of Music and the Christian Church* (Westport, Ct. and London: Greenwood, 1996), 137.

4. Steven R. Guthrie, "Singing, in the Body and in the Spirit," *The Journal of the Evangelical Theological Society* 46/4 (December 2003): 633-646.

5. John Calvin, *Institutes of the Christian Religion*, ed. John T. McNeill (Philadelphia: Westminster, 1960) book IV, chapter XIV, no. 1, The Sacraments, 1277.

6. "Symbol," The American Heritage Dictionary, 3rd ed. (New York: Dell Publishing, 1994), 820.

7. R. J. Gore, *Covenental Worship: Reconsidering the Puritan Regulative Principle* (Phillipsburg, N.J.: P&R Publishing, 2002) 72, 73.

8. Calvin, *Institutes*, book IV, chapter 14, no. 10.

9. James F. White, *Introduction to Christian Worship,* 3rd ed. (Nashville: Abingdon, 2000), 194.

10. 1 Peter 3:18-21

11. "Chapter 14. Christian Assembly on the Lord's Day," The Didache, www.earlychristianwritings.com/text/didache-roberts.html (accessed January 10, 2006).

12. 1 Corinthians 10:16, 17

13. Acts 20:7; 1 Corinthians 16:2

14. Revelation 1:10v

15. Matthew 26:26; Mark 14:22; Luke 22:19, 24:30, 35; Acts 2:42, 46; 20:7, 11; 27:35; 1 Corinthians 10:16; 11:23

16. Dom Gregory Dix, *The Shape of the Liturgy* (New York: Seabury, 1945), 82-86.

17. Didache, chapter 14.

18. Thomas B. Falls, *The Fathers of the Church: A New Translation,* vol. 6, The Writings of Justin Martyr (Washington: Catholic University of America Press, 1948), 106-7.

19. Robert E. Webber, *Evangelicals on the Canterbury Trail: Why Evangelicals Are Attracted to the Liturgical Church* (Harrisburg, Pa.: Morehouse, 1985), 43.

20. Ibid., 47.

21. Ibid., 48.

Chapter 6, Denominational Ethos

1. Robert Webber, in his *Complete Library of Christian Worship*, vol. III (Nashville: Star Song, 1993), 121, explains that Psalm 95 provides the biblical underpinning for this theory. The psalm begins with a call for loud shouts to God, but by verse 6 moves on to humble bowing in worship.

2. The "subscriptionist" issue currently debated in more conservative Reformed denominations revolves around how fully one must adhere or "subscribe" to these foundational confessions of the church.

3. Hugh Thomson Kerr, ed. *A Compend of Luther's Theology* (Philadelphia: Westminster Press, 1943), 146.

4. Martin Luther, *Luther's Works,* vol. 53, *Liturgy and Hymns*, ed. Ulrich S. Leupold (Philadelphia: Fortress, 1965), 321-324.

5. Data collected from e-mail interviews conducted by the author with the admissions office and music department, November 21, 2003.

6. E-mail interviews conducted by the author with admissions office and music department.

7. Luther, *Luther's Works,* vol. 40 (Philadelphia: Muhlenberg Press, 1958), 95-100.

8. Luther, *Luther's Works,* vol. 40, ed. by Jaroslav Pelikan, Hilton Oswald, and Helmut Lehmann (St. Louis: Concordia, 1955), 119, 147.

9. Ibid., vol. 51, 84.

10. Ibid., vol. 40, 91, 99.

11. Ernest B. Gilman, *Iconoclasm and Poetry in the English Reformation: Down Went Dagon* (Chicago: University of Chicago Press, 1986), 35.

12. Johann Eberlin von Gunzburg, *Ain fraintlich trostliche vermanung an alle frummen Christen, zuo Augspurg am Leech* (Wittenberg, Germany, 1522?). These and other such images may be viewed by accessing the Kessler Digital Image Archive Collection at the Candler School of Theology, Emory University, Atlanta.

13. Paul Corby Finney, *Seeing Beyond the Word: Visual Arts and the Calvinist Tradition* (Grand Rapids: Eerdmans, 1999), 12.

14. Information booklet accompanying compact disc J. S. Bach, *Epiphany Mass*; Paul McCreesh, conductor; Archiv Production #457 631-2.

15. Personal interview conducted by the author with Dr. Hawkins, January 16, 2006.

16. Statistic from a denominational survey conducted by George Barna in 2001; see Web site www.adherents.com (accessed January 17, 2006).

17. Bard Thompson, *Liturgies of the Western Church* (Philadelphia: Fortress, 1961), 295.

18. Charles E. Hambrick-Stowe, "Ulrich Zwingli: Prophet of the Modern World," *Christian Century*, April 4, 1984, 335.

19. Review of CD *Zurich, Arise* in *American Record Guide*, May/June [2000?], 257; see www.guildmusic.com/reviews/rev7175z.htm.

20. William H. Halewood, *Six Subjects of Reformation Art: A Preface to Rembrandt* (Toronto: University of Toronto Press, 1982), 5.

21. R. J. Gore, *Covenantal Worship: Reconsidering the Puritan Regulative Principle* (Phillipsburg, N.J.: Puritan and Reformed Publishing, 2002), 9.

22. Richard Hooker, Washington State University, www.wsu .edu/ ~dee/REFORM/ZWINGLI.HTM.

23. The philosophical/theological concept of dualism has its roots in Plato, in whose thought the material world is seen as a mere copy or shadowy form of reality. True reality exists only on the spiritual level, according to Plato, and therefore material things are considered less desirable, or even evil.

24. Sign Value refers to the degree to which a given liturgical act, especially a symbolic one, properly and accurately represents that which it signifies. For example, it may be asked: to what degree do the amount and use of water in a baptismal service properly and accurately signify the theological baptismal themes of death and resurrection or cleansing from sin?

25. James F. White, *Protestant Worship: Traditions in Transition* (Louisville: Westminster John Knox, 1989), 61.

26. John Calvin, *Commentaries on the Book of Genesis,* vol. 1 (Grand Rapids: Baker, 1981), 217.

27. Calvin, *Institutes,* book IV, chapter 10, section 14.

28. Ibid., section 30.

29. John Calvin, *Commentary on the Book of Psalms,* vol. 2 (Grand Rapids: Baker, 1981), 494. See also Calvin's commentary on Psalms 81:1-3 and Psalm 71:22.

30. *Nunc Dimitis* is the Latin translation of the first two words of Simeon's Prayer, found in Luke 2:29-32. This and other biblical poems found outside the book of Psalms are referred to as canticles and are frequently sung in Christian churches.

31. Barbara Kiefer Lewalski, *Protestant Poetics and the Seventeenth-Century Religious Lyric* (Princeton: Princeton University Press, 1979), 215.

32. Lukas Vischer, ed., *Christian Worship in Reformed Churches Past and Present* (Grand Rapids: Eerdmans, 2003), 20.

33. See Part III of Vischer's *Christian Worship in Reformed Churches Past and Present.*

34. Paraments are the cloth hangings from pulpit, lectern, and altar/table, or hanging on the wall behind an altar.

Chapter 7, Reflections from an English Cathedral

1. Picture taken from the Web site *Salisbury Project*, www3.iath.virginia.edu/salisbury/docs/cathedral.html (accessed January 10, 2006). Used by permission of Marion Roberts.

2. From Web site *Salisbury Project.* Used by permission.

3. Edward Rutherfurd, *Sarum: The Novel of England* (New York: Ivy Books, 1987).

4. Ibid., 506.

5. Photo used by permission of Dave Stewart, Department of History, Hillsdale College, Hillsdale, Mich.

6. Photo used by permission of Dave Stewart.

7. Ernest B. Gilman, *Iconoclasm and Poetry in the English Reformation* (Chicago and London: University of Chicago Press, 1986), 31.

8. How intriguing (and typical of human nature) that artwork, supposedly to be made "utterly extinct and destroyed," somehow ends up instead getting loaded into boats for France. Apparently, business was business in the sixteenth century as well as in our own.

9. Gilman, *Iconoclasm and Poetry*, 7-9.
10. William H. Halewood, *Six Subjects of Reformation Art: A Preface to Rembrandt* (Toronto: University of Toronto Press, 1982), 4.
11. Ibid., 11.
12. Photo obtained through the courtesy of Robert Seitz.

Chapter 8, Roadblocks to Holistic Worship

1. Arthur W. Pink, *Exposition of the Gospel of John*, 3 vols., (1923; repr., Grand Rapids: Zondervan, 1968), 206-209.
2. Barry Liesch, *People in the Presence of God: Models and Directions for Worship* (Grand Rapids: Zondervan, 1988), 154.
3. Ibid., 271.
4. Donald Hustad, *True Worship: Reclaiming the Wonder and Majesty* (Carol Stream. Ill.: Hope, 1998), 67, 68.
5. Ibid., 63.
6. George Barna, *Real Teens: A Contemporary Snapshot of Youth Culture* (Ventura: Regal Books, 2001), 17.
7. Ibid., 60.
8. Robert E. Webber, *The Younger Evangelicals: Facing the Challenges of the New World* (Grand Rapids: Baker, 2002).
9. Ibid., 189-190
10. Ibid.
11. Ibid., 67.
12. Ibid., 61.
13. Colleen Carroll Campbell, *The New Faithful: Why Young Adults Are Embracing Christian Orthodoxy* (Chicago: Loyola Press, 2002).
14. Ibid., 85, 86.
15. Robert Webber, *Evangelicals on the Canterbury Trail.*
16. Franky Schaeffer, *Sham Pearls for Real Swine* (Brentwood, Tenn.: Wolgemuth & Hyatt, 1990).
17. Thomas Howard, *Evangelical Is Not Enough: Worship of God in Liturgy and Sacrament* (Fort Collins, Colo.: Ignatius Press, 1988).
18. Webber, *Evangelicals on the Canterbury Trail*, 15, 16.
19. Ibid., 24, 25.

Chapter 9, The Well-Tempered Worship Service

1. Traditional expository preaching starts with and expounds upon a passage of Scripture, as opposed to topical preaching, for example, which starts with and expounds upon a particular topic. Verse-by-verse expository preaching, as the name indicates, gives an ordered and detailed analysis of the biblical passage one verse at a time.

2. The reproduction of the labyrinth on the floor of Chartres Cathedral in France is used by permission of Jacques Hébert of Quebec, who manages the Web site www.labyreims.com/ e-chartres.html.

Selected Bibliography

Best, Harold M. *Unceasing Worship: Biblical Perspectives on Worship and the Arts.* Downers Grove, Ill.: InterVarsity Press, 2003.

Blackwell, Albert L. *The Sacred in Music.* Louisville: Westminster John Knox, 1999.

Bradshaw, John L., and Norman C. Nettleton. *Human Cerebral Asymmetry.* Englewood Cliffs, N.J.: Prentice-Hall, 1983.

Calvin, John. *The Library of Christian Classics, Vol. XX: Institutes of the Christian Religion.* Philadelphia: The Westminster Press, 1960.

Campbell, Don G. *Introduction to the Musical Brain.* 2nd ed. St. Louis: MMB Music Inc., 1983.

Carroll, Colleen. *The New Faithful: Why Young Adults Are Embracing Christian Orthodoxy.* Chicago: Loyola Press, 2004.

Dix, Dom Gregory. *The Shape of the Liturgy.* New York: Seabury Press, 1945.

Doran, Carol, and Thomas H. Troeger. *Trouble at the Table: Gathering the Tribes for Worship.* Nashville: Abingdon Press, 1992.

Dyrness, William A. *Visual Faith: Art, Theology, and Worship in Dialogue.* Grand Rapids: Baker Academic, 2001.

Finney, Paul Corby. *Seeing Beyond the World: Visual Arts and the Calvinist Tradition.* Grand Rapids: Eerdmans, 1999.

Forrester, Duncan, and Douglas Murray. *Studies in the History of Worship in Scotland.* Edinburgh: T & T Clark LTD, 1984.

Gore, R. J., Jr. *Covenantal Worship: Reconsidering the Puritan Regulative Principle.* Phillipsburg, N.J.: P&R Publishing, 2002.

Howard, Thomas. *Evangelical Is Not Enough.* Nashville: Thomas Nelson Publishers, 1984.

Hustad, Donald P. *True Worship: Reclaiming the Wonder and Majesty.* Wheaton, Ill.: Harold Shaw Publishers (Hope), 1998.

Leithart, Peter J. *From Silence to Song: The Davidic Liturgical Revolution*. Moscow, Idaho: Canon Press, 2003.

Liesch, Barry. *People in the Presence of God: Models and Directions for Worship*. Grand Rapids: Zondervan, 1988.

Meyers, Jeffery J. *The Lord's Service: The Grace of Covenant Renewal Worship*. Moscow, Idaho: Canon Press, 2003.

Ornstein, Robert, and Richard F. Thompson. *The Amazing Brain*. Boston: Houghton Mifflin, 1984.

Saliers, Don E. *Worship as Theology: Foretaste of Glory Divine*. Nashville: Abingdon Press, 1994.

———. *Worship Come to Its Senses*. Nashville: Abingdon Press, 1996.

Springer, Sally P., and Georg Deutsch. *Left Brain, Right Brain*. Revised ed. New York: Freeman and Co., 1985.

Storr, Anthony. *Music and the Mind*. New York: Ballantine Books, 1992.

Sweet, Leonard. *Post-Modern Pilgrims: First Century Passion for the 21st Century World*. Nashville: Broadman and Holman, 2000.

Thompson, Bard, ed. *Liturgies of the Western Church*. Philadelphia: Fortress Press, 1961.

Vischer, Lukas, editor. *Christian Worship in Reformed Churches Past and Present*. Grand Rapids: Eerdmans, 2003.

Walton, Janet R. *Art and Worship: A Vital Connection*. Collegeville, Minn.: The Liturgical Press, 1991.

Webber, Robert E. *Evangelicals on the Canterbury Trail: Why Evangelicals Are Attracted to the Liturgical Church*. Harrisburg, Pa.: Morehouse, 1985.

White, James F. *Protestant Worship: Traditions in Transition*. Louisville: Westminster John Knox, 1989.

The Vital Worship, Healthy Congregations Series

John D. Witvliet, Series Editor

Published by the Alban Institute in cooperation with the
Calvin Institute of Christian Worship

BOOKS IN THE SERIES

C. Michael Hawn
One Bread, One Body:
Exploring Cultural Diversity in Worship

Norma deWaal Malefyt and Howard Vanderwell
Designing Worship Together:
Models and Strategies for Worship Planning

Craig A. Satterlee
When God Speaks through Change:
Preaching in Times of Congregational Transition

Peter Bush and Christine O'Reilly
Where 20 or 30 Are Gathered:
Leading Worship in the Small Church

Robert P. Glick
With All Thy Mind:
Worship That Honors the Way God Made Us

With All
Thy Mind